Not a Mile
From
Milk Street

Sundridge

drawn by Hilary Vickers

Fig. 1 The Crown, Plaistow

Courtesy: Bromley Central Library

Not a Mile from Milk Street

a short history of St Andrew's parish, Bromley

by Andrew J. Martin

First edition edited by William Burford

Second edition edited by Patrick Pearson

To

Ann-Marie

who tolerated annexation of the dining table and lengthy spells at the laptop more or less stoically

And

In memory of my Great Uncle George Hammond, who died aged 27 on 29th August 1918 and my Great Nephew Finlay Joseph Martin aged 4, who died on 20th January 2011. Both, divided by four generations, went before their time.

First published in Great Britain 1982

2nd Edition (Revised): 2012 published by the author

ISBN 978-0-9508704-1-0

Printed and bound in Great Britain by TJ International Ltd., Padstow, Cornwall

Proceeds from the sale of this hardback book will go towards the building of the new St Andrew's Community Hall in Burnt Ash Lane, Bromley, Kent

The Author, Andrew Martin (L)
and Editor, Patrick Pearson

Contents

List of Illustrations

Foreword

to the 1ˢᵗ Edition

by the Bishop of Rochester, Rt Rev. Dr R D Say

Rochester Cathedral was originally dedicated to St Andrew and for long centuries the Bishop of Rochester lived in Bromley and was the owner of land now in the parish of St Andrew. So it is a special pleasure for me to welcome Mr Andrew Martin's fascinating history of St Andrew's, Bromley, and to commend it to all those concerned with the life of the local community. Lord Evershed, a former Master of the Rolls, once wrote: 'The child of today will be the citizen of tomorrow, and every boy and girl will be a better member of the local community in which he or she lives, if imagination has been fired in youth by the ancient records of which that community is justly proud. We cannot hope to plan successfully for the future unless we first understand the past.' I believe that this book will help many to understand the past history of the community in which they live and to see how many different strands have been woven together to make up the busy place we all know today. Everyone will find something to interest them in this carefully researched and interesting history. Some may think that the list of landlords of 'The Prince Frederick's Head' is an unusual feature in such a book! But publicans, as well as priests and policemen, have contributed greatly to local life down the years, along with many others. I hope this book will be widely read and that it will take its rightful place in the archives of both parish and borough.

David Roffen:

Bishop R D Say on a visit to
St Andrew's on the occasion of
the Golden Jubilee of the parish, 1980
Photo: Andrew Martin

Foreword
to the 2nd Edition
By the Bishop of Rochester, Rt Rev. James Langstaff

Bishop David Say, the 104th Bishop of Rochester, in his foreword to the first edition commented that 'many different strands have been woven together to make up the busy place we know today'. In producing his second edition Andrew Martin has drawn on many more. I have been privileged to visit St Andrew's parish on several occasions during the past two years as the 107th Bishop of Rochester and have come to know a few of its people. Bishop David spoke of publicans, priests and policemen who have contributed to the life of the community over the years, and following on from this, Mr Martin refers to places, people and presence in this extended work. Place names tell us something of the past and help us understand the history of an area. People are so important in the developing life of a place or community. Many may have gone unremembered, but again Mr Martin has highlighted some who have made a valuable contribution to their community and their country. Finally there are those organisations mentioned in this volume whose very presence not a mile from Milk Street help foster and support the heart beat of local life to be found in church, chapel and community engagement for the better of all.

Andrew Martin, as a local person, has delved deeply into the life and health of this community and the results of his research deserve to be widely read.

+ James Roffen:

Bishop J Langstaff
Courtesy: Diocese of Rochester

Introduction to 1st Edition

It is perhaps tempting to assume that an apparently young newly developed area of a town like Bromley hasn't got a history.

The Sundridge Park district has been transformed in a short space of less than a century from a predominantly pastoral landscape to a densely populated suburb of London. Land ownership has passed from a handful of substantial estates to several thousand private house-holders and in part to the Local Government Authority.

Sundridge itself has passed from the Scott family and via a hothouse of executive endeavour, the Sundridge Park Management Centre to its present metamorphosis as Sundridge Park Manor, a rather splendid period hotel complete with crystal chandeliers and terraced lawns.

Plaistow Lodge, which has a fascinating history, is no longer in private hands, but is now home to the Parish C of E Primary School.

William Hicks, who was to distinguish himself as Sir William Joynson-Hicks Bart, Home Secretary, lived at Plaistow Hall, another substantial house in the district, since demolished.

Newcomers to the Sundridge Park area of Bromley may not know of the existence of Springhill, another ancient house standing on Plaistow Green (Fig. 12) This book identifies the oldest buildings in the district and briefly tells the story of several, like Sundridge Hall which have come and gone.

No little time was spent on the search for information on the 'Prince Frederick' in Nichol Lane, whose history appears to date back several centuries.

We then trace the history of the parish of St Andrew's from its early beginnings at the mission rooms in the parish of St Mary's through to the dedication of the present church in 1930 and onto the present day.

Introduction to 2nd Edition

For reasons, I suppose, of lack of time, the first edition contained only brief references to the effects of the two world wars on the local area. I have tried to redress the balance in the 2nd Edition.

Those who perished in the Great War are commemorated on the wayside shrine in St Andrew's church. It was only after looking closely at it that I realised that so many of those who fell were in the same regiment, the Queen's Own Royal West Kents, as my own great-uncle George Hammond who, aged 27, shared the same fate and was killed on 29th August 1918 at Bancourt, near Bapaume, Picardie and is laid to rest at Vis-en-Artois military cemetery, 15 km east of Arras.

However, relating the names on the shrine to the local area is fraught with difficulties almost a century on. Using available military records I have tried to identify as far as possible where those who fell in the Great War lived. Sadly, about 65% of service records of those who fought in WW1, held at Hounslow, were destroyed by enemy action during the Blitz.

One of the practical difficulties is that the fact that a name appearing on a head-stone in a cemetery in England is no guarantee that the deceased is buried there. It has been the custom to add the name of war dead, or missing, to family head-stones as a memorial to the deceased. The familiar CWGC headstones may indicate that the individual is buried there or they may be memorials in name only of individuals lost or buried in some theatre of war. The Borough Council does, of course, hold detailed records for every grave.

During World War II the area was severely affected both by the loss of a significant number of members of the forces on active service and, locally, as the result of enemy bombing. Apart from sporadic bombing from 1940 onwards resulting in the loss of life, there was extremely severe targeted bombing during the Blitz especially in April 1941 with heavy loss of life in Southover, Nichol Lane, Lansdowne Road and Babbacombe Road on the night 16th/17th April. On the same night the Parish Church of SS Peter and Paul, Bromley was also razed to the ground, except for its tower. Then later there was again loss of life in June 1944 when a bomb fell on Treewall Gardens.

It is already nearly a century since so many made the ultimate sacrifice in the Great War and close to 70 years since the end of World War II. Inevitably the once-familiar names of those who made that sacrifice have become less distinct. I hope that in identifying most of those from the local area who gave their lives in both world wars, and other conflicts, and as far as possible tracing their families and addresses, at least they will be more readily remembered in the years to come. I am acutely aware of the possibilities of errors in identification of individuals.

I have also sketched in information on some of the people and events that have shaped the area over the years since the 1st Edition was published.

The book is not, and is not intended to be, comprehensive in coverage. It is still a 'short history', so its brevity may explain any perceived omissions, but not the inevitable errors for which I apologise. So far, since its first appearance in 1982, this book has been revised at 30-year intervals regularly, like clock-work. The author would like to make it clear that there is no guarantee that it will be re-issued in 30 years' time so speculation on the likely appearance of NAMFMS 3 in 2042 is not recommended.

AJM

Acknowledgements (1ˢᵗ Edition)

Many people have provided information and assisted with compiling this book. I would especially like to acknowledge the assistance of Bill Burford who was responsible for editing it; Geoffrey Eames for valuable information from his own work and from the archives of St Mary's, Plaistow; Miss Silverthorne, Miss Plinke and the staff of Bromley Central Library Local History Department; the staff of the Guildhall Library, City of London; Miss E Rose Muncey, Mr Toley Cooper and Mr L Burbridge for the loan of photographs; the National Portrait Gallery for permission to reproduce the Dandridge portrait of Prince Frederick; Hilary Vicars (Holy Trinity Convent) for her drawing of Sundridge (frontispiece); Mr S Goad for taking photographs; Mr G Church for preparing the map illustrating the Apportionment of Rent Charge in lieu of Tithes (1841); Mrs K Goodwin, Mr R Ridgeway, Mrs J Cooper, Mrs C Luffman, Mrs M Wain, Rev. Preb. R Cason, Mrs D Viner, Mr F W J Burford and Mrs N A Farris for notes on the Organisations; Mr R Woolgar and Mrs Hooper for notes on the Brook Lane Chapel and the Rangefield Mission; Mrs D Murray for notes on Bromley and Downham Boys' Club; to those who by giving their personal support made publication possible; to Mr N Bate for guidance and assistance with the design and production and last and by no means least to Mrs H Jones and Mrs A Dulley for much typing from the original hieroglyphics, and to all others who helped in any way.

AJM

Acknowledgements (2ⁿᵈ Edition)

I would again express my thanks

to Arthur Holden, Simone Harris and the staff at Bromley Central Library, Local Studies Section whose unfailing expertise and enthusiasm enable obscure information to be traced with lightning speed;

to Peter and Mary Fall (who incidentally follow in the footsteps of Rev. Gowans in upholding the standards of musicianship at St Mary's, Plaistow) and to Peter Boyden and others at St Mary's for responding patiently to my requests for information;

to niece Lucy Gahagan for the cover design and digitally reconstructing a badly damaged photo of St Andrew's Mission Church (Fig. 19) and to niece Rebecca Rosel who arrived unexpectedly from Melbourne to work on mapping and pictures;

to Sir Tim Berners-Lee for inventing the world-wide web in time for the 2nd edition (I wish he had got his act together in time for the first), and to his offspring Messrs Google, Google and Google for saving a lot of leg-work;

to the Commonwealth War Graves Commission, for their tireless efforts to make the key information on war casualties publicly and freely available on-line. The work of an amateur sleuth like myself would be virtually impossible without their dedicated and thorough work, undertaken quietly and efficiently over many years. No praise could be too high for this achievement;

to Giles Guthrie and the staff at the Queen's Own Royal West Kent Regimental Museum at Maidstone, for willing assistance and advice;

to Dale Copley at the Royal Fusiliers Regimental Museum, HM Tower of London for access to the regimental archives;

to Rosie Applin and the staff at Christ's College, Cambridge for their contribution relating to Prof. Frank Spooner;

to Linda Lee-Wright, St Peter's College, Oxford for solving the riddle of the Christopher Chavasse portrait;

to George and Alan Church for their wartime memories, and to George for his excellent drawings;

to Thelma Dulley, amongst her many interests, a volunteer at the London Metropolitan Archives and indefatigable researcher into family history, for tracking down obscure genealogical information;

to Doris Burford for photographs from her archive and to Joan Harrison for assistance with the identification parade;

to Jenny Chambers for kindly giving permission for reproduction of her late brother's sketch of Igor Stravinsky;

to Helen Smith (Women's Guild), Bruce Manning, Kate Allen, Sue Elwood, Emma Povey and others (25th Bromley Scout Group), Greg Smith and Phil Wilcox (BADA), Phil and Hilary Cheverton (Bromley & Downham Youth Club) and various other people for notes on their respective organisations;

to the present clergy at St Andrew's, Revs. Angela King and Liz Davis for their encouragement and practical contributions to the text and to Canon Peter Cole and Rev. Anthony Atherton for filling in some of the gaps;

to Bill Lea for assisting in a survey of Plaistow Cemetery, to identify the graves and memorials to the war dead;

to Tony Isbitt of Tony Isbitt Photography for kind permission to reproduce his work;

to Patrick Pearson; print-wiz, actor, baritone and all-round polymath* for his unstinting support and hawk-eyed attention to anything falling below his exacting standards;

to the many other people who have so willingly and freely assisted with the preparation of this book, and as far as humanly possible, I have tried to acknowledge all original sources of text and illustrations. For any errors or omissions I crave your indulgence.

*Tautology Ed

AJM

Lestrade,
St Junien la Bregère,
23400 Creuse, France

1
Woodlands and Farms

For the late twentieth century resident it is difficult to imagine the 'Burnt Ash' area of Bromley as a stretch of unspoilt countryside. But two hundred and fifty years ago in the area which is now the parish of St Andrew there were very few dwellings of any description.

The Rocque map of 1744[1] shows a substantial area of woodland. Mosel Heath Wood lay to the east of Burnt Ash Lane in the area which is now Ridgeway Drive and Broadlands Road and Strafield Wood was on the opposite side stretching up to the present Westminster School playing fields. To the west of Strafield Wood lay Keedon Wood. Burnt Ash Lane is shown on the map but not named. However, the area to the north of what is now Grove Park is identified as 'Burndish'. The Rocque map is not an accurate document and 'Burndish' is likely to be a corruption of 'Burnt Ash'.

Approximately in the position of the present New Street Hill was Shonstock Hill Lane which extended into Empstead Lane, and in turn joined the Mottingham to Chiselherst (sic) road. Milk Street is clearly marked together with a lane which appears to follow the route of the footpaths still existing in 1982 between Hall's Farm House, Milk Street and New Street Hill in one direction and from the farm to Garden Road in the opposite direction.

In 1723 William Pasenger had a survey of his land undertaken by John Holmes Jnr. A splendidly detailed map prepared following the survey is preserved in the archives of Bromley Central Library (Fig. 2). From the acreages shown in the index to the index to the map, it can easily be deduced that William Pasenger's house was that on Plaistow Green closest to the junction between Nichol Lane and the road to Widmore. The house next door is undoubtedly Plaistow Hall, and thereafter moving clockwise round the green are Springhill and Plaistow Lodge. The Lodge would have been the original building prior to rebuilding which commenced in 1777. The road we now know as Burnt Ash Lane was indicated on the survey map as Riddens Lane (leading to the wood known variously as Riddens, Riddons or Riddles Wood). Ownership of land around the green was in the hands of John Know, Yeoman, Arnold King, Gent., John Knightly, Esq., Thomas Simons, Yeoman, and William Pasenger himself. Elsewhere in the district, land was in the hands of John Washer Esq., Roger Peck, Gent., John Steeven Esq., and The Lord Rumney.

---

[1] Rocque map of 1744 (Bromley Central Library)

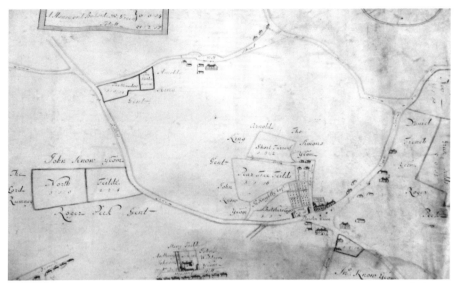

Fig. 2 Survey of the lands of Wm. Pasenger 1723   *Courtesy: Bromley Central Library*

According to the index to the map, Pasenger owned London Lane Field, the two Broom Fields, the two New Green Fields, Short Furrow, Pear Tree Field, Butcher's Croft, the two North Fields, the three Gore Fields and a field called Brook. In addition he owned land and dwellings occupied by others as follows, In Gaston's (Gasion's?) hands, a garden and meadow adjoining; in William Bath's hands, a house barn and orchard etc.; in William Wicker's hands, one piece called Bell Mead; in Mr Dutton's hands, a house and orchard etc.; in Mr Inocent's hands a house, yard and garden etc and in Mr Waldron's hands a house, bakside etc.

By 1723 the first dwellings in Nichol Lane had appeared as, is believed, had the timber ale-house known as the 'Prince Frederick's Head' (see ch.3). Apart from these one could have walked from Plaistow Green towards Lee along the narrow winding tree-lined Burnt Ash Lane without coming across any sign of human habitation.

The nearby hamlet of Plaistow was described by Thomas Wilson in 1797 as 'certainly a rural, retired spot, but when you have seen the few gentlemen's houses that are in it, nothing remains deserving notice, the rest being hovels, and the inhabitants poor; but content often takes up her abode in a cottage'. By the mid-nineteenth century the land was essentially arable or laid to pasture and land ownership was dominated by the estates dealt with in detail in the next chapter. The Apportionment of the Rent Charge in lieu of Tithes in the Parish of Bromley of 1841 gives a precise indication, not only of the ownership of all the land in the parish of Bromley, but also of its exact utilisation in that year (Fig. 6)

The map shows that the western part of the parish was substantially owned by Robert Boyd the freeholder of Plaistow Lodge. The stream which rises at the end of

Brook Lane and crosses Upper and Lower Brooks Meadow marks the boundary between Boyd's land and the six fields in the parish owned by Sir Thomas Baring. Thus Alexandra Crescent was built on land formerly part of the Plaistow Lodge Estate and eventually sold for residential development by Lord Kinnaird at the turn of the 20th century. Rangefield Road and all the houses on the Downham Estate to the North of Brook Lane including the whole of Southover (to the north of the Rangefield Road junction) was built on land owned by Sir Thomas Baring, who has given his name to the Baring Hall public house at Grove Park. However the remainder of Southover and Rangefield Road stand on land owned by the heirs of Thomas Morgan in fields named Further Noble Field and Hither Noble Field.

The whole of Powster's Hill, the site of the Bromley Reservoir above Thornton Road, Hillcrest Road and the land now occupied by Westminster School Playing Fields were owned by the Bishop of Rochester. The Chatsworth Avenue and Welbeck Avenue area and land now developed to the west of Burnt Ash Lane north of Kynaston Road was owned by the Heirs of Thomas Morgan. Land to the east of that part of Burnt Ash Lane, the south end of both Ridgeway Drive and New Street Hill were owned by the Bishop of Rochester; Treewall Gardens, Broadlands Road and the central part of Ridgeway Drive are within the boundary of Riddles Wood owned by George Ward Norman, was by 1841 under the plough. The most northerly part of Ridgeway Drive adjoining Burnt Ash Lane was owned by John Lee.

The part of the Links Estate, now crossed underground by the River Quaggy, including Oaktree Gardens, Leamington Avenue and Portland Road, and the rising slope of New Street Hill was in the hands of the Heirs of Thomas Dowley and at the summit of the hill the two fields known as Great New Street and Little New Street now occupied by the top of Portland Road were owned by Sir Samuel Scott. The extreme easterly corner of the parish, now part of Grove Park Cemetery, bordering on Elmstead Woods comprised three fields known as Great Marvels, Bushy Piece and Hornbeams.

Rotunda House (formerly the site of 'The Teasel') together with the Church Army Housing development stand on former pasture owned by the Bishop of Rochester, as does the Sundridge Parade of shops. Between the end of the shops and the rear of the gardens on the east side of Southover lay a long narrow field known as North Field and this land became Roslin Way.

In 1841 the only roads in the parish were Burnt Ash Lane, Hollow Bottom (Nichol Lane), Milk Street, Mottingham Lane (New Street Hill), and Brook Lane. The Milk Street housing development stands on Brick Kiln Field to the north of Milk Street and on land formerly owned by Sir Samuel Scott to the south. Vale House Farm once stood on the south side of Milk Street and the Southern Railway Line eventually separated Vale House Farm from Hall's Farm, which still stands together with a pair of semi-detached cottages.

Nursery Ground, Sawpit Field and Hunt's Field, all owned by Sir Samuel Scott, became the land which, combined, became King's Meadow, Plaistow Cemetery and the site of St Andrew's Church, the church hall and St Andrew's House. Lags Land, lying opposite North Field was developed in the early twentieth century to become Gladwell Road and Hilldrop Road. The houses in Burnt Ash Lane from its junction with Gladwell Road to Croft Road stands on Foxley Field, and those in Foxbury Road, Croft Road and Foxbury Close on three fields owned, like Foxley Field, by the Heirs of Thomas Morgan. Minster Road stands partly on Green Field and partly on the former orchard at Hollow Bottom.

The eight houses in Nichol Lane opposite the Prince Frederick have given way to new development, and the four cottages which were the only houses of any description in Burnt Ash Lane have been replaced by the present Nos. 2 and 4 Burnt Ash Lane.

Hollow Bottom itself was by far the most densely populated area of the parish in 1841! Apart from the eight cottages there was a house adjoining the right hand side of the Prince Frederick occupied by William Peacock and two terraced houses to the left of the pub owned by the landlord, Richard Addis. George Marshall lived at the detached cottage (now No. 27 Nichol Lane) and Thomas Gander opposite.

So, in 1841 what did the area look like? Assuming the arable land to be cornfields, standing in Alexandra Crescent amongst the corn, looking towards Powster's Hill you would see two copses in front of you beyond which there were two meadows crossed by the brook, with cornfields rising up Powster's Hill to the summit. Climbing the hill and looking down towards Milk Street, you survey a mixture of pasture and arable land with narrow tree-lined Burnt Ash Lane meandering through the countryside. In the valley slightly to your left the lush grassland surrounding the river Quaggy is separated by cornfields which cover the slope as it rises to Elmstead Woods at the top of New Street Hill.

Next door to the farm, in the direction of Bromley, was a residential house known as Sundridge Hall owned by Archibald Deloford who kept a riding stable, his ponies occupying the fields alongside Burnt Ash Lane below Powster's Hill. Deloford's house fell into disrepair and was finally demolished with some assistance from the younger gentlemen of the parish after the second world war. The only picture traced so far is of a bedroom in the Old Hall which at least gives the flavour of the style of the building. (Fig. 4) The site became waste land known locally as the Delly Fields and eventually became the location of Waitrose, the supermarket at one end, and 'The Teasel' (now demolished) at the other.

The farm house in Milk Street is surrounded by orchards and gardens with a large pond in the meadow nearby. Strolling along the lane to Plaistow Green you see pastures to your left and the wooded grounds of Mr Boyd's mansion to your right

Fig. 3a Hall's Farm House, Milk Street   *Courtesy: Bromley Central Library*

Fig. 3b Milk Street, leading to Hall's Farm House   *Postcard Courtesy: Chris Hoskins*

Rounding the bend into Nichol Lane you make your way to the 'Prince Frederick's Head' for a jug of ale and across the bar you pass the time of day with Richard Addis, mine host of a pub which already in 1841 has stood there at least since midway through the previous century!

In 1861 Hall's Farm in Milk Street was occupied by the forty-year old John Barrett, the shepherd, his wife Catherine and four children, Emma, Noah, Hannah and George, ranging in age from thirteen to three.

The only other cottages, numbers 2 and 3 Milk Street were occupied by Richard Marshall, an agricultural labourer, his wife Elizabeth, and their 14-year-old nephew Thomas, a domestic garden boy at No. 2, and Richard Adams a retired worker, his wife Elizabeth and their 19-yearold niece Charlotte Roach at No. 3. In Redden Wood lived John Holt with his wife Harriet and two baby daughters. A small community which has come and gone is Sundridge Hall, Sundridge Hall Farm and the farm

Fig. 4 Sundridge Hall, Burnt Ash Lane   *Courtesy: Bromley Central Library*

cottages. The farm was built in the late 1860s and in 1871 was occupied by James Cowie a Scotsman farming 150 acres. His wife, at 42, 21 years his junior and 19-year-old daughter Mary were assisted in the running of the farmhouse by three servants, Mary Palmer, Alice Howard, both Londoners, and Eileen Harris from Limerick. The farm stood in Burnt Ash Lane opposite the end of Mottingham Lane now New Street Hill). In the 1920s Mr Withycombe, proprietor of the Bromley Cab Company, who operated horse-drawn cabs from the Bromley Railway Stations, grazed his horses on the pasture alongside Burnt Ash Lane. The farm house was demolished around 1933 but the cowsheds continued to be used by Groom's the bakers, whose horse-drawn delivery vans were a daily feature around the district.

Perhaps the single most significant event which transformed the face of the countryside, and led to massive residential development, was the advent of the railway link to London. The 1870 and 1874 Ordnance Survey maps show the first railway line to cross the area which was the South Eastern line running via the tunnel beneath Elmstead Woods. There was no station between Hither Green and Chislehurst. The railway line linking Grove Park Station with Bromley was opened on 1st January, 1878.

6

Fig. 5 Hadlow's Garage on the corner of Nichol Lane and Plaistow Lane with Nichol Lane
to the left   *Courtesy: Bromley Central Library*

The first mention of Gladwell Road appears in Strong's Directory for 1904, with Arthur Fisher occupying No. 1 and Augustus Rands at No. 2. By the following year five families had moved into the street, and houses numbered up to 23 existed. By 1905 houses in Hilldrop Road had been completed up to No. 21, and ten families had moved in.

Many people have wondered about the origin of the name Burnt Ash. We cannot do better than quote from History of Lee and its Neighbourhood by F H Hart, published in 1882. He says, 'The origin of "Burnt-ash" was in consequence of the felling of timber formerly grown in the woods, the lopping and roots of which were burnt for the manufacture of charcoal for sale in London. Burnt Ash Farm contained many areas of Woodland. In the year 1823, the farmer, Mr William Wiggins grubbed up the woods near where St Mildred's Church now stands, and burnt charcoal'.

The farm stood at the south-west corner of the junction of the present Baring Road and St Mildred's Road, but in those days would have been approached by that same leafy lane from Plaistow Green to Lee.

In what must have been one of the first signs of colonization Fig. 7 shows an isolated 3-storey villa with no other apparent signs of habitation. This is No. 3 Burnt Ash Lane, still there in 2012 (Fig. 8), standing back from the road as you skirt round from Plaistow Green at the top of Burnt Ash Lane with the lane winding away in the back-ground. Later, during the war, this house must have looked out on the devastation caused by the bombing of Nichol Lane in 1941.

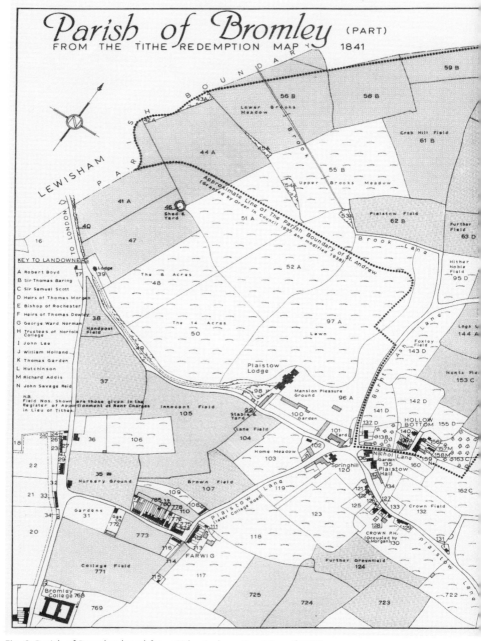

Fig. 6 Parish of Bromley (part) from Tithe Redemption Map of 1841

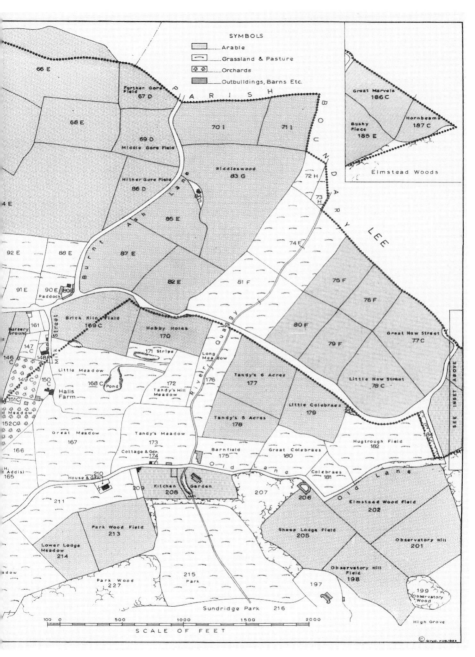

SYMBOLS

Arable
Grassland & Pasture
Orchards
Outbuildings, Barns Etc.

66 E

Further Gore Field
67 D

68 E

69 D
Middle Gore Field

Hither Gore Field
86 D

85 E

4 E

92 E

88 E

87 E

91 E

90 E

Paddock

161

Nursery Ground

147 C

148 C

146 C

149 C

150 C

151 C

152 C

166

Brick Kiln Field
169 C

Halls Farm

168 C Pond

Little Meadow

Great Meadow
167

Tandy's Meadow
173

Cottage & Gdn.
174

H. (Addis)
165

House & Gdn.

211

210

209

Park Wood Field
213

Lower Lodge Meadow
214

Park Wood
227

Hobby Holes
170

171 Stripe

172

Tandy's Hill Meadow

Long Meadow

176

Barnfield
175

Kitchen
208

Garden

215
Park

197

Sundridge Park   216

70 1

71 1

Riddleswood
83 G

72 H

73 H

74 F

82 E

81 F

80 F

Tandy's 6 Acres
177

Tandy's 5 Acres
178

Great Colebraes
180

Little Colebraes
179

Colebraes
181

207

206

Sheep Lodge Field
205

Observatory Hill Field
198

75 F

76 F

79 F

77 C
Great New Street

78 C
Little New Street

Hugtrough Field
182

Elmstead Wood Field
202

Observatory Hill
201

199
Observatory Wood

High Grove

SEE INSET ABOVE

Great Marvels
186 C

Bushy Piece
185 E

Hornbeam
187 C

Elmstead Woods

P A R I S H   B O U N D A R Y

L E E

Burnt Ash Lane

Mill Street

River Quaggy

Old Lane   Lane

Old

100 0   500   1000   1500   2000

SCALE OF FEET

Drawn by George Church

9

Fig. 7 Burnt Ash Lane, early 20th Century   *Courtesy: Bromley Central Library*

Fig. 8 Still there in 2012 (without the pony and trap)   *Photo: Andrew Martin*

2

The Estates

Sundridge Park – Plaistow Lodge
Plaistow Hall - Springhill

There were several estates or substantial houses which dominated the northernmost area of Bromley in terms of land ownership and no doubt employment. These included Sundridge, Plaistow Lodge, Plaistow Hall, Springhill and later Freelands.

The Apportionment of the Rent Charge in lieu of Tithes in the Parish of Bromley (Fig. 6) reveals the extent of the land holdings by the estates in 1841. These showed major holdings by Sir Samuel Scott, resident at Sundridge, Robert Boyd of Plaistow Lodge (later Quernmore School), George Ward Norman and the heirs of Thomas Morgan. The Scotts of Sundridge were active in the affairs of St Mary's Plaistow and it was through their co-operation that land was eventually made available for the building of the St Andrew's 'Tin Church'.

In 1874 there was discussion in Bromley concerning the acquisition of a new cemetery. The Rev. Angus MacFarlane[2] records that the then vicar of St Mary's, Mr Hodgson, called a meeting to discuss the matter, but a curious situation arose when no-one turned up. The feeling was that there was room enough in the church yard for another twenty years. Eventually after some acrimonious discussion a site for a new cemetery was agreed from Lady Scott's estate in Burnt Ash Lane, the agreed price being £550 per acre. The cemetery, which was laid out for 3,443 graves, was dedicated by the Bishop of Dover in 1893.

The Sundridge Estate undoubtedly came into the hands of the Scott family in 1796 when it was bought by Claude Scott of Chislehurst (later Sir Claude Scott Bart) from Edward George Lind. However other land appears to have been acquired by Scott and added to the estate. Horsburgh[3] states that 'Antiquarian research has not succeeded, so far, in tracing the land tenures of this locality further back than the early sixteenth century, but it is known that in 1500 one estate with house attached was in the hands of a family named Ryder 'of Battersey and Bromley', the estate, which was situated on what was then known as Milk Street, passing before 1589 into the hands of the King family, which retained possession until 1754.

---

[2] *St Mary's First Hundred Years 1863-1963*

[3] *Bromley, Kent from the Earliest Times to the Present Century* by ELS Horsburgh (1929)

The property was then sold to a Mr Jones Raymond, ultimately coming into the hands of the Scotts of Sundridge Park. A portion of the land was, in early days, the property of the influential Knight family, who parted with that part of it on which Springhill now stands to Arnold King. The land on which Plaistow Hall was subsequently erected is thought, by Mr B F Davis, to have been under the possession of the Shott family in the sixteenth century, though other authorities think it more probable that this piece also belonged to the Kings.'

Sundridge

Hasted (Vol 1 p 559)[4] says (language modernised):

'Sundridge is a manor and seat, situated towards the north-east corner of this parish (of Bromley), among the woods, and was formerly the residence of a noted family of the name of Blund or Blound, who were anciently lords of Guines in France. One of these had three sons who came into England with William the Conqueror; of these, one returned into France again, and the other two, Sir Robert and Sir William, remained in England, the former settling in Suffolk, and the latter in Lincolnshire. From these the several families of Blount in this Kingdom are descended. Of a younger branch of them was Peter le Blund, who was owner of this place in the reign of King Henry III in the 39th year of which (1254) he was made Constable of the Tower of London. His descendant, Edward de Blund, was possessed of Sundridge, in the 20th year of King Edward III (1346) as appears by the book of aid for that year; in which Edward de Blund was assessed for one quarter of a Knight's fee, which John de Blund before held in Broomleigh of the Bishop of Rochester'

Horsburgh elucidates further (p.191) 'In that year (1346) on the occasion of conferring knighthood upon the King's eldest son - it was the year of Crécy and the initiation of the Black Prince into the arts of war - a requisition up to 40s on every Knight's fee was made by order of the King. A transcript of the accounts of the collectors was made many years later by Cyriac Petit in the 35th of Henry VIII, (1543) and therein under the title "Hundred of Bromleigh and Bekenham" there appears this entry of Edward de Blound, for one quarter of one fee, which John de Blound held in Bromleigh of the Bishop of Rochester - xs."

Horsburgh queries whether Hasted had evidence that Peter de Blund owned Sundridge in 1254, and claims that the first documented proof of ownership by the Blund family appears to be from the *Pedes Finium* preserved in the Record Office.

He says "From this document it appears that a certain Henry of Gloucester and Margaret his wife put in a claim against John Le Blunt, draper of London, to the

[4] *The History and Topographical Survey of the County of Kent* by Edward Hasted, published 1797-1801

possession of 'the Manor of Sundresshe, near Brumleigh', which claim was arbitrated in the King's Court at York in the 30th of Edward I (1301) with the result that "the aforesaid Henry and Margaret his wife acknowledge the aforesaid Manor with the appurtenances" to be the right of the said John." They therefore abandon all claims to it for themselves and for their heirs. In consideration of their acknowledgement, John le Blunt "gave to the same Henry and Margaret the sum of Twenty pounds sterling"

Horsburgh says (p. 191)

'A few years after the death of Edward de Blound, Sundridge appears as the property of Robert Forneaux "citizen and fishmonger of London" and it passed by the marriage of his widow to Andrew Pykeman, also a citizen of London and a

Fig. 9 Sundridge Park   *Courtesy: Bromley Central Library*

member of the same city company. Pykeman died in 1391 leaving the property to his daughter, whose husband, John Sibile, thus became the owner. She died in 1401 and his property was left in the hands of his three sons, Thomas being the one who lived at Sundridge, where he died in 1421. A short time later Sundridge is found to be the property of Ralph Booth.'

Hasted's account parts company with Horsburgh.

Hasted has it that

'John Blund's family (at an unstipulated date) ended in a female heir, who carried the seat in marriage to Willoughby; from which name it passed by purchase, to Booth, whose descendant, William Booth, was found by inquisition taken in the first year of King Henry VII (1485) to die possessed of the manor of Sundrigg, held of the Bishop of Rochester, as of his palace of Rochester, by Knight's service, and by the service of making suit at the court of the palace, and that Robert Booth was his son and heir, who was, with one hundred other gentlemen of this country, made Knight's of the Bath, in the l7th year of that reign (1501) in whose descendents Sundridge continued till Sith Booth Esq., dying without male issue . . . . . ."

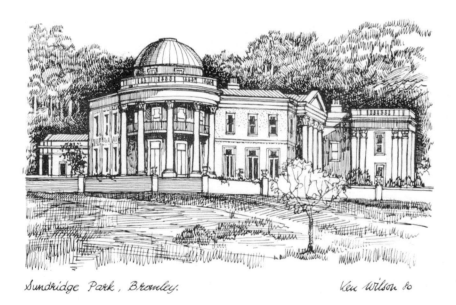

Sundridge Park, Bromley.   Ken Wilson 80

Fig. 10 Sundridge Park, drawn by the late Ken Wilson, architect of Bromley Central Library and Churchill Theatre   *Courtesy: Bromley Central Library*

The path by which Sundridge eventually came into the hands of the Scott family in 1796 is shown on the chart which also indicates the difference between the accounts of Hasted and Horsburgh.

14

Ownership of Sundridge

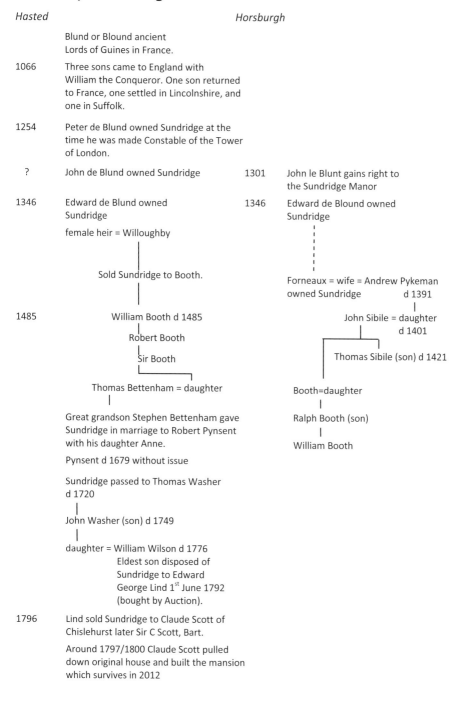

Hasted   *Horsburgh*

Blund or Blound ancient Lords of Guines in France.

1066 Three sons came to England with William the Conqueror. One son returned to France, one settled in Lincolnshire, and one in Suffolk.

1254 Peter de Blund owned Sundridge at the time he was made Constable of the Tower of London.

? John de Blund owned Sundridge

1301 John le Blunt gains right to the Sundridge Manor

1346 Edward de Blund owned Sundridge

1346 Edward de Blound owned Sundridge

female heir = Willoughby

Sold Sundridge to Booth.

Forneaux = wife = Andrew Pykeman owned Sundridge   d 1391

1485 William Booth d 1485

John Sibile = daughter
                    d 1401

Robert Booth

Thomas Sibile (son) d 1421

Sir Booth

Thomas Bettenham = daughter

Booth=daughter

Great grandson Stephen Bettenham gave Sundridge in marriage to Robert Pynsent with his daughter Anne.

Ralph Booth (son)

Pynsent d 1679 without issue

William Booth

Sundridge passed to Thomas Washer d 1720

John Washer (son) d 1749

daughter = William Wilson d 1776
Eldest son disposed of Sundridge to Edward George Lind 1st June 1792 (bought by Auction).

1796 Lind sold Sundridge to Claude Scott of Chislehurst later Sir C Scott, Bart.

Around 1797/1800 Claude Scott pulled down original house and built the mansion which survives in 2012

15

Describing Bromley in 1797 T Wilson[5] refers to Sundridge House, late the elegant seat, beautiful park and extensive pleasure grounds of William Wilson Esq., and says that 'the estate including the manor and a pretty villa now in the occupation of George Dubois Esq., were sold by an auction on 1st June 1792 for £18,000 to George Lind Esq., and in 1796 resold to Scott Esq., (sic) of Chislehurst who is building a new house on this truly enchanting spot. (Wilson refers to Claude Scott the first member of the family to occupy Sundridge). This clearly dates the building of the present house, known in the locality as 'The Mansion' (Figs 9 & 10), at the turn of the 18th century. The Scott estates extended beyond the bounds of the parish of Bromley.

F H Hart[6], writing in 1882 said

'At the South end of Marvels lane, and facing the Bromley road, is Grove Farm, now called Grove-park which was formerly the property of Thomas Waller, Esq., wine merchant of the City of London. It was sold by the executors of that family to Mr John Pound, for building purposes. It contained about sixty-eight acres of meadow and arable land, the frontage of which, on the Bromley road, has been nearly all covered within the last few years with charming villas, which are near to the Grove-park Railway Station. Here is a new road made, running to the extreme end of Lee parish, adjoining the property of the late Sir Samuel Scott, the eminent banker, of Cavendish-square, London, and Sundridge-park, Bromley. About fifty acres of this estate is in the parish of Lee, and forms the southern boundary. Much of this land was formerly wood, known as Riddon's Wood, and was well stocked with game, and famous in hot weather for snakes, lizards, and adders.

Fig. 11 Plaistow Lodge: Ravensbourne School, Quernmore Annex in 1982; The Parish C of E Primary School in 2012   *Photo 1982: Andrew Martin*

---

[5] An accurate Description of Bromley by Thos Wilson, printed for Thos Wilson, Bookseller, Bromley
[6] History of Lee and its neighbourhood

Plaistow Lodge

According to Horsburgh:

'The Plaistow Lodge estate extending to 126 acres stretched northwards from the present London Lane and contained all the lands to the west of Burnt Ash Lane. The property did not become a single estate until well into the eighteenth century, the owners in 1675 - the earliest date to which tenures have been traced - being three members of a family named French. Passing through several hands, either by inheritance or purchase, the whole property was bought in 1777 by Peter Thellusson, a gentleman who had accumulated an enormous fortune estimated at £800,000 of which he spent £40,000 in erecting the present mansion known as Plaistow Lodge, Fig. 11 (later Quernmore School). The sudden rise in rateable value of the estate, from £84 in 1777 and succeeding years, to £175 in November 1796, was evidently the consequence of the construction of Plaistow Lodge.

"After the death of Peter Thellusson early in 1797, his widow, Anne, remained in possession until 1804, when presumably upon her death, the ownership passed to Peter Isaac Thellusson, son of the original Peter. In 1806 he became the first Baron Rendlesham in the Irish peerage, and in all probability retired from the south to the Thellusson estates in Yorkshire. At any rate in 1810 Plaistow Lodge was leased by the Thellusson trustees to a Mr Thomas Maltby, and two years later the whole estate was purchased from the trustees by the Hon. Hugh Lindsay of the family of Crawford and Balcarres. In 1822 Mr Lindsay in turn sold it to William Boyd, or rather to a group of grateful clients who presented it to Mr Boyd as a token of gratitude and esteem, at a cost of £17,000.

'This remarkable man, whose life is traced in the Dictionary of National Biography, was a banker and financier of great repute who was born in or about 1754. He had large interests in Paris, where he was residing at the outbreak of the French Revolution. There he remained, refusing to seek refuge at home for ten years, safeguarding as far as possible the interests of his clients, of his creditors and of his bank. It was in acknowledgement of these services that Plaistow Lodge was presented to him at the conclusion of the Napoleonic Wars. During his residence at Plaistow Lodge the place was well kept up, and it is said that fifty persons slept under its roof every night. Open house to tradesmen and others was practically the rule in the servants' quarters, and it was no uncommon thing to hear three or four fiddles going in the servants' hall of an evening.

'On Walter Boyd's death in 1837 the Estate passed to his son, Robert Boyd, who held it to his death in 1863. From 1869 to 1873 the Estate was held by Mr J Mackenzie who sold it in 1873 to the Hon. Arthur Kinnaird. In 1878, on the death of his brother, the ninth Baron, he succeeded to the Barony, residing at Plaistow Lodge till his death in 1887.

'He was succeeded in turn by his eldest son Arthur Fitzgerald Kinnaird, who then became the eleventh Baron. In 1896 Lord Kinnaird ceased to reside at Plaistow Lodge. He resolved to break up the estate and to destroy it as a residential centre. The house itself, with a sufficiency of surrounding land, was leased by Mr Gustav Loly, who transferred to the palatial and commodious situation the boys' school known as "Quernmore", originally established by Mr John Gibson in Holwood Road.'

The house (Fig. 11), later Quernmore School then the Quernmore Annexe to Ravensbourne School for Boys is currently the Parish C of E Primary School, a large primary for 450 pupils formed by the amalgamation of Parish School and St Mary's Primary School in 1987. The Parish School was inaugurated in 1771 on the site of the present Bromley Methodist Church at the top of College Road near Bromley College.

So from its roots in the two previous schools the Parish C of E Primary School now resident at Plaistow Lodge in London Lane has a proud tradition of 240 years of C of E-based education.

Plaistow Hall

The third estate at the Northern end of Bromley was Plaistow Hall, now demolished, a substantial red brick building situated opposite the point where Cambridge Road meets Plaistow Lane. Horsburgh writes 'On its site a house appears to have stood long before the erection of the hall, the property in the sixteenth century being either part of the Shott Estate, or that of the King family. The tenures have been successfully traced through a Henry Molls, who sold to Andrew Broome in 1597; in 1605 the estate was sold by Andrew Broome to Henry Walton, and from the Walton family it passed in due course to Peter Burrell who built Plaistow Hall about 1700. Peter Burrell sold to Richard Swift, and from the latter, the property was acquired by William Passinger (elsewhere spelt Pasenger). Ultimately it passed into the hands of the Scott family of Sundridge, who had as tenants of Plaistow Hall one of the Boyds, and later a Mr Kincaid, from whom the remainder of the lease was taken over by Mr William Sewell Shuttleworth, who, at its expiration renewed it for twenty-one years.

Mr Shuttleworth died in 1863, and his widow remained in occupation until 1882. 'Mr Shuttleworth was a great figure in Plaistow.

His memory, as a philanthropist and friend of the poor still survives:

> "Friend of the poor, beloved of friends, and dear
> To all who knew thy worth, and felt how near
> Thy kind heart beat to poor man's wants and ways
> And how, with open hand, thou cheer'st their days."

'Such was his fitting obituary contributed to the Bromley Record in 1863. His Christmas present to the poor in 1858 was three bullocks, with a corresponding supply of bread and soup. His eldest son Wm Yorke performed the extraordinary feat of riding a bicycle from Russia to Calais, in order to disprove the opinion "that a religious zealot must be a muff".

'From 1885 Plaistow Hall was in the hands of Mr Henry Hicks whose son, William was a somewhat conspicuous figure in the Bromley of my day' (Horsburgh was writing during the period 1925-9). He varied an assiduous devotion to his business as a solicitor in London with an equally assiduous devotion to the cause of "Protestantism" as against the High Churchman. "I am a Prot" he once said to me, and for a moment I was at a loss to recognise the particular sect to which he thus proclaimed his attachment. He gave the impression of a man who meant to get on in the world, and Sir William Joynson-Hicks Bart MP and Home Secretary, has justified the promise of his youth.

It was the same William Hicks who ran St Andrew's mission hall situated across the road from Plaistow Hall in the grounds of Plaistow Lodge. Plaistow Hall was eventually demolished in 1900.

Springhill

Horsburgh (p. 186) says

'From ancient times there seems to be a house and a farm on the site of Springhill. It was a part of the possessions around Bromley of the Knight family from whom it was bought by Arnold King early in the seventeenth century. It remained in the hands of the King family throughout that century, or the greater part of it. A Robert King sold to a Mr Walsingham King, who in turn sold to Roger Peck in 1712. The deed cementing this sale describes the house as a very ancient one. This ancient house in due course disappeared, to be replaced by the present structure, but the precise date of the present house and the name of the man who caused it to be built are alike unknown, but if in 1857 it was in fact, as it was reputed to be, about 150 years old that would carry back its origin to Walsingham King or Peck.

'About the middle of the last century the property was divided, roads being made to enable the fields to be turned into a building estate. The house itself with its surrounding gardens was bought by Mr Edwards who lived there for some years, but in 1857 Mr Edwards sold it to Major Clement Satterthwaite of the Stock Exchange, who resided at Springhill for over 30 years.'

Major Satterthwaite was a great benefactor of St Mary's Church, Plaistow. He enlarged the house and during his time Cambridge Road and adjacent roads came into existence. In 1888 the ownership of Springhill passed to Mr John Gordon and later to Mr William Bowley (1895-6), and to Miss Bowley (1896-9). After a vacancy Springhill was acquired by the Kent County Council as a school for domestic economy.

Springhill served as an auxiliary fire station during WW2. The fire station took a direct hit on 2nd November 1940, when two firemen were killed.

Amidst a great deal of public concern and some scepticism the building was declared to be in dangerous condition and it was finally demolished in 1967. The site of Springhill is the grassed roundabout at the junction of Burnt Ash Lane, College Road, Plaistow Lane, London Lane and Cambridge Road. The area was formerly known as Plaistow Green. Incidentally the meaning of 'Playstow' is 'village green mainly for recreation'.

Fig. 12 Springhill   *Courtesy: Bromley Central Library*

3

'The Prince Frederick'
and Hollow Bottom

Hollow Bottom, now Nichol Lane, is a fascinating spot which has almost, but not quite, changed out of all recognition. It is certainly one of the oldest residential streets in the parish of St Andrew's.

The Rocque map of the area (1744)[7] indicates three dwellings in Hollow Bottom, which at that time was a cul-de-sac running from Plaistow Green and extending as far as the footpath which still connects Nichol Lane with Minster Road and thereafter to Hall's Farm and New Street Hill. The map is however not generally accepted as reliable, and perhaps a more authentic document is a map of the immediate area drawn up following a survey of the lands of William Pasenger Esq., undertaken by John Holmes Jnr, in 1723 (Fig. 2). This clearly shows two houses on the site of the 'Prince Frederick' on land owned by Thomas Symons, Yeoman, and two houses opposite, one owned by John Haile and the other occupied by 'Bromley Poor'. These were the only houses in Hollow Bottom, but there were other houses grouped around Plaistow Green. The hamlet was commonly known as Hollow Bottom until relatively recently, with the Ordnance Survey map of 1912 (Fig. 20) identifying it as such. There are two houses of considerable interest in the lane; number 27 (in 1982 named Hollow Bottom cottage) and 'The Prince Frederick' itself.

Who was Prince Frederick?

The public house in Nichol Lane was named after Prince-Frederick, Prince of Wales who lived from 1707 to 1751 (Fig. 13). Frederick Lewis was the elder son of George II, born to George and Caroline of Anspach in 1707 during the reign of George I.

When George II became King in 1727 there was already an appalling relationship between both George and Caroline and Prince Frederick. His mother is reported to have said of her son 'my dear first-born is the greatest ass, the greatest liar, the greatest canaille and the greatest beast in the whole world and I heartily wish he was out of it'.

---

[7] Bromley Central Library Archives.

Fig. 13 Prince Frederick, Prince of Wales
by B Dandridge
Courtesy: National Portrait Gallery

The King created him the Prince of Wales on 9th January, 1729 but sought to keep him out of a position of influence by cutting his allowance to £24,000 per year, a quarter of what he himself received when he was Prince of Wales. Not to be denied, the Prince continued to patronise the Italian opera, and held court with politicians, wits and dramatists who sought his company.

He was a keen patron of the arts, and as an expression of that patronage he commissioned the building of one of the most splendid state barges still in existence. Prince Frederick's barge designed by the architect William Kent is housed in the National Maritime Museum at Greenwich.

The Prince used the barge on the day it was launched in 1732 to take the Queen, the five Princesses and himself from Chelsea Hospital to Somerset House attended by officers and ladies in another barge, and a 'Set of Musick' in a third. From then on, the barge was in constant use on trips frequently concerned with Poetry and music. After the Prince's death in 1751 the vessel became the principal royal barge, and was used by successive monarchs until 1849 when Prince Albert was rowed to the opening of the Coal Exchange.

The King allowed Frederick to marry, choosing the 17-year-old Princess Augusta of Saxe-Gotha, and continued to ostracize both son and daughter-in-law. Despite this the prince's popularity grew by leaps and bounds. 'My God' said the King 'Popularity always makes me sick, but Fretz's popularity makes me vomit'. Frederick hit back by describing the King as an obstinate self-indulgent miserly martinet with an insatiable sexual appetite.

The war which broke out in 1739, first against Spain and then against France as well, was wholeheartedly supported by Prince Frederick. Walpole resigned on 1st February 1742 but the Prince was outmanoeuvred by the King who reconstructed the government by retaining some of the existing ministers and by installing some of the Prince's professed friends in positions of power. The King's popularity rode high when he went into battle at Dettingen on what proved to be the last occasion a reigning monarch risked his life fighting alongside his soldiers. This popularity was much needed when the Young Pretender invaded Britain in 1745, taking Edinburgh, Carlisle and Derby before being overtaken by the King's troops.

'Poor Fred' had spent his life telling people what he would do when he succeeded his father, but it was he who was to die first, in March 1751. He died suddenly at Leicester House, on 20th March, 1751, from the bursting of an abscess which it is thought had been formed by a blow from a real tennis ball.

He was buried on 13th April 'without either anthem or organ' in Henry VII th's Chapel in Westminster Abbey. The King put up a somewhat unconvincing display of sorrow at his eldest son's death and adamantly refused to pay his debts. Prince Frederick was father, by his wife, of the future King George III and a further four sons and two daughters. He also had a son Cornwell Fitz-Frederick by Anne Vane ('Beautiful Vanella'); this son is also buried in Westminster Abbey.

At the end there was considerable public disaffection with the Hanoverians illustrated by a lampoon written at the time:
The Prince of Wales' epigram (quoted by William Makepeace Thackeray, *"Four Georges"*):

> "Here lies poor Fred who was alive and is dead,
> Had it been his father I had much rather,
> Had it been his sister nobody would have missed her,
> Had it been his brother, still better than another,
> Had it been the whole generation, so much better for the nation,
> But since it is Fred who was alive and is dead,
> There is no more to be said!"

The 'Prince Frederick's Head'

Guildhall Library records clearly identify the 'Prince Frederick's Head' in a register of fire insurance policies of the Hand-in-Hand Fire and Life Insurance Society dated 28th January 1761 (Fig. 15) The text reads:

> 'Thomas Symons of Mason's Hill near Bromley in Kent Wheelwright £150 on a Timber House etc. Valued as per Margin on the East Side of Nicholls's Lane at Plaistow in the parish of Bromley, County of Kent. Known by the Name of the prince Frederick's Head Ale House and in the Possession of Henry Burbridge. Renewed January 30th 1768 per Samuel Cooper.'

The calculations in the margin show a valuation of £140 for the house, £8 for the brew house and £2 for the shed over the cellar stairs. The description indicates an ale-house of timber construction, thus predating the present brick-built structure.

The fire insurance policy was renewed at seven-year intervals until it expired in 1789 when no renewal was made. In 1768 the freeholder was evidently Samuel Cooper of Farnborough, Kent, and Henry Burbridge was still the occupier. By the time the policy was renewed for a further period of seven years in 1775 Henry Burbridge had died and his widow Sarah was registered as both the occupier and the owner. According to the register the policy premium of 2s 3d per year appears to have been paid annually from 1782 until the payment for the year to January 1789.

What happened to the alehouse during the 43-year period from 1789 to 1832 is not clear, but it is interesting to note that the fire insurance policy for the adjacent cottage was maintained by a renewal paid on January 18th 1796 presumable expiring in January 1803. This cottage is the present No. 27 Nichol Lane (Fig. 14a) which is the last house to survive modern development in Nichol Lane and is almost certainly the oldest dwelling in the parish. Several bricks in the exterior walls bear the date 1739, almost certainly indicating the date of building (Fig. 14b).

In 1761 Thomas Symons was owner of both the 'Prince Frederick's Head' and the cottage, with Ann Draper occupying the cottage. By 1768 Samuel Cooper had become owner of both properties and ownership of the cottage had changed again by 1775 when Sarah Burbridge is registered as the owner. Ann Draper continued to occupy the cottage, but by 1782 it was apparently vacant. Between 1782 and 1789 entries indicate the fire insurance premiums of 1s 6d were paid annually, and a renewal was made on January 20th 1789 by Ann Hoar, a spinster, of Church Street Deptford, but no occupant is listed.

There is an interesting entry in the Fire Insurance Society's register for January 18th 1796 in which the clerk began to make the statement from previous entries that the house was the First house to the North of the 'Prince Frederick's Head', then crossed it out and simply referred to it as 'a dwelling house to the north . . . indicating that other houses had been built just prior to 1796. These are apparently the two cottages referred to in the Apportionment of The Rent Charge in lieu of Tithes of 1841. The original cottage was referred to in 1796 as, late in the possession of Wooton'.

Pigot's London and Provincial Directory was first issued in the early 1820's. The edition of 1823-4 lists seven taverns and public houses in Bromley. These were the 'Bell Tap', the 'Duke's Head', the, Greyhound', the 'Rising Sun', the 'Rose and Crown', the 'Star and Garter' and the 'Three Compasses'. No mention was made of the 'Prince Frederick, in this edition nor in the edition of 1826-7.

Hollow Bottom must have been so remote from Bromley as to have escaped the notice of the compiler. However, the 'Prince Frederick' does appear in the edition of 1832-3-4 with Richard Addis as the landlord and he remained there at least until 1855 in which year *Kelly's Directory* identifies him as the landlord of the public house and as a farmer.

Fig. 14 a Hollow Bottom Cottage

Fig. 14b '1739' carved in brick

Photos: Andrew Martin

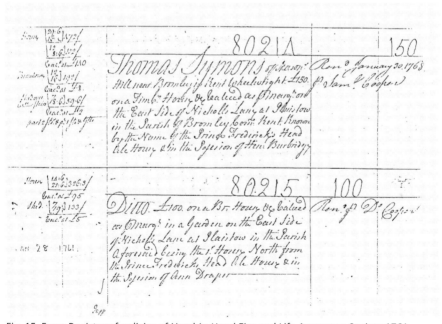

Fig. 15 From Register of policies of Hand-in-Hand Fire and Life Assurance Society 1761

Courtesy: Guildhall Library

Fig. 16 The 'Prince Frederick', 1890   *Courtesy: Mr Toley Cooper*

The Apportionment of the Rent Charge in lieu of Tithes in the Parish of Bromley of 1841 shows Richard Addis farming arable land owned by John Lee. He also rented Riddles Wood and a cottage adjacent to the wood from George Ward Norman. Riddles Wood was to the east of Burnt Ash Lane were Broadlands Road and Ridgeway Drive are now. Richard Addis also rented a barnyard and orchard and a meadow from the heirs of Thos. Morgan as well as Pear Tree field. From the same owner the rented pasture and Foxley Field, a name obviously very close to Foxbury

Road built much later in the immediate locality. His own property in the parish comprised the public house itself and two adjoining terraced cottages since demolished, situated between the public house and the present cottage No. 27 Nichol Lane. Richard Addis was 45 in 1841 and he and his wife Harriet had four children - William (22), Edward (19), John (12) and Jane 9. According to the first National Census of 1841 there were 35 households in the lane and one unoccupied house. In Hollow Bottom there were a total of 180 men, women and children, including about 30 labourers (general, builders' and agricultural) and others listed as carpenters, gardeners, grooms, blacksmiths, sailors, man-servants, an army private, a mealman and a grocer (the publican).

In 1866 John Wallis was the landlord and no doubt he was in business with Ezekiel Kelsey who lived in one of the other houses in Hollow Bottom and was listed in Strong's Directory for the year as a brewer and coal merchant. In 1870 or 1871 Henry Whittington took over and between 1874 and 1876 his place was taken by Joseph Fullex. William Frisby remained for two years in 1877 and 1878 when R Knight moved in and stayed for thirteen years until 1890. 1890 is the year in which the pub was substantially rebuilt and received its new frontage. Messrs H & V Nicholls Ltd undertook extensive alterations including the addition of a tap room and pot house to the left of the original building and new internal walls dividing the ground floor into a public bar, private bar and private parlour. The bar parlour was to the rear (to be replaced in 1926 by a club room) and a kitchen in the position now occupied by the rear of the saloon bar.

The frontage of the building was almost entirely replaced on the line of the old frontage, the only part remaining unaltered being the three first floor windows to the right of the building (see Fig. 17). Discovery of a photograph dated February 10th 1890 (Fig. 16) reveals that the building was developed in at least three separate stages. In 1890 it was no longer the timber building described in the insurance records of the late eighteenth century. The adjacent cottage to the left of the pub is clearly of Kentish weather boarding and demolition of this cottage made way for the tap-room (now the public bar). So sometime during the nineteenth century the pub was rebuilt in brick. Although permission was granted in April 1890 the application also had to go before the Bromley Brewster Sessions and the Bromley Record for October 1st 1890 reported the application.

The Chairman had evidently been to see the premises and said that the alterations consisted of acquiring the cottage next door and converting it into a tap room. The only objection he saw was that a door opened into a side passage which

The list of landlords is shown below:

1761 - ca 1775	Henry Burbridge	1896 - 1901	William Jayes
ca 1775 * ca 1789	Sarah Burbridge	1902 - 1904	C A Dawson
ca 1789 - 1832	Not known	1905 – 1913	J B Botterill
ca 1832 - ca 1855	Richard Addis	1914 - 1916	William Chas Harcourt
ca 1855 –ca 1871	John Wallis	1918 - 1919	William Jas Haddon
ca 1871 – ca 1875	Henry Whittington	1920 - 1932	Albert H Button
ca 1875 - 1877	Joseph Fullex	1933 - 1934	Albert F Ashwell
1877 - 1878	William Frisby	1935 - 1951	Harry Chas Hawes
1878 - 1890	R Knight	1951 - 1961	Toley Cooper
1891 - 1893	William Snelgrove	1961 - 1975	Thomas Atkins
1894 – 1 895	Edward Walker	1975 -1983?	James Kirby

would give facilities for serving drink during prohibited hours. Mr Gregory for the proprietor promised that the door would be blocked in and the alterations were allowed.

William Snelgrove, who had been living next door but one to the pub since 1876, evidently acquired it in 1891 and ran it until 1893. William Snelgrove was the Great Grandfather of Bill Burford who in 1982 lived in the same cottage in Nichol Lane (now No. 27) occupied by his Great Grandfather over a century before.

Albert Button's wife was still remembered (in 1982) by the longest standing customers of the 'Prince Frederick' for being permanently drunk and her husband forbade her from entering the pub. Not to be outdone she lowered her jug on a string out of the front bedroom window for sympathetic customers surreptitiously to fill and return.

The exact date the original 'Prince Frederick's Head' was built is not yet established. It was certainly not later than 1761 as evidenced by the Hand-in-Hand insurance policy. Thomas Symons, who owned the alehouse in 1761, already owned the land and two houses on it in 1723. There is no reason to believe that the pub was not one of those houses. But is it possible that the alehouse existed long before the time of Prince Frederick and was re-named? And what is the origin of the name Nichol or Nicholls? A search into the deepest recesses of Bromley Library archives reveals the existence of documents in Latin and English granting licences to certain men of Bromley. One of these licences was granted to a John Nicholes, victualler in the year 1605! The records are those of the Justices of the Peace for the Upper Division of the Lathe of Sutton-at-Hone including the Hundreds of Blackheath, Bromley and Beckenham, Litle and Lesnes and Ruxley.

The licence reads as follows (from the Latin):

'Memorandum that on the 5th day of September in the 3rd year of the reign of our illustrious Lord, King James of Scotland, England etc, John Nicholes of Bromley in the aforesaid county (Kent), victualler, came before us, Timothy Lowe, Knight, Samuel Leonard, Knight, and Edmond Style Esq., three of the Justices of the peace of our said Lord the King for the said country. He appeared personally before us at Bromley and he bound himself in the sum of £10 and Nicholas Giles of Bromley aforesaid, butcher, and Godfrey Lamme of Bromley aforesaid, husbandman also came and stood surety for the aforesaid John Nicholes in the sum of £5 each, which sums of £10 and £5 they acknowledge that they owe to our Lord the King to be charged on their lands, tenements, goods and chattels for his use and that of his heirs and successors if the aforesaid John Nicholes defaults on the conditions set out below.'

The code of conduct the alehouse keeper was required to observe makes fascinating reading. Here are a few snippets:

CONDICIONS FOR AN ALEHOUSE LICENCE 1605[8] The condicion of the Recognizances is such That Whereas the above bounden stand severally admitted and allowed by his Majesty's Justices above named to keepe Common alehowses or Tipling howses .... lodginge for passengers and wayfaringe men And doe not keepe in their howses or permitt to be broughte into their howses any dice cards or tables nor suffer any play in theire howses yard or backside att Cards dice or tables, or other unlawfull games And doe not suffer any minstrelsey or dancinge in or about their howses And doe not dresse or suffer to be dressed or eaten within their howses any fleshe upon any day forbidden by the lawes and constitucions of this Realme except to persons lawfully lycenced therto .... And do not suffer any person to resort remayne and continewe in theire said howses that is notoriously suspected of fellony, or that is indicted or notoriously suspected to be an unlawfull hunter of Deare or conies by nighte or by day or to be a taker of phesants or partriges contrary to the statuts in that behalf or that is a common alehowse haunter drunckard or quarreller or of incontinent lief or any other Riotuous Idle Roguishe or beggerly people And doe not suffer any drunkennes in theire howses nor any excessive quafinge by the dozen yard bosshell or other disordered manner but shall forth with informe the nexte Justice of those riotuous persons that doe attempte to committ any such disorder in theire howses .... And doe not Brewe in their howses but take their drinke from the brewer where it may be so had and the best to be put at vis the barrell and the smale at iiiis the Barrell And doe sell and drawe oute theire drinke by the ale quarte or pinte and nor by Judgs and cups and sell the best after iiid

---

[8] Bromley Central Archives (1b)

the ale gallon and the worst after the rate of iid the ale gallon and that such as must needs brewe them selves doe make it soe that they may sell it at the price aforesaid And doe not suffer any person or persons to lodge in their howses above a day and a nighte but such as they will answere for and shall make the Constable or other officer pryvie therto And doe not buy or take to pawne the goods of any way fayinge men or other that shall bringe the same to their howses to sell but of such as shalbe well knowen unto them to be of honest conversation and whome they shalbe well knowen unto them to be of honest conversation and whome they shalbe hable to produce or have alwaies to be forth cominge ………Then every of theis Recognizances to every person hereby above bounden and named so observinge and performinge the same To be void and ineffectuall and to the reste to remayne and in full power and vertue'

So was John Nicholes, victualler, of Bromley in the year 1605, the man who gave his name to the Nichol Lane of 2012 and the Nicholls Lane of 1761? What could have been more appropriate than to have named the lane which led to the victualler's alehouse after the keeper himself? But in which part of Bromley did he have his abode? Was it Plaistow?

The parish records of St Peter and Paul, Bromley (the Parish Church) date back to 1558 for christenings, January 1575/6 for marriages and 1578 for burials. Unfortunately, prior to about 1670, the records are no more specific concerning place of birth or domicile than 'Bromley'. Thereafter it is generally possible to pinpoint localities such as Plaistow, Widmore and Emstead more precisely. So whereas the Plaistow families French, Washer, Burbridge, Simonds, Lambourne, Onwyn, Draper and others from 1670 onwards can be positively identified we cannot, from these records, say with certainty that John Nicholls was a resident of Plaistow.

However we can piece together the family tree and this is shown below. He married Agnes Newmisse in 1579 during the reign of Elizabeth I and had a son and three daughters. His first daughter Mary died in infancy. The second daughter Elizabeth married Samuel Frenneby and the third, born in 1591/2 was probably one of the two Ann Nicholls who died within a few months of each other in 1624.
His only son James married Dennys Cosin in 1607 and had four daughters, two of whom died in infancy. James' second daughter married Richard Burbridge, a name which from then onwards features in the registers with increasing frequency (either as Burbidge or Burbridge). When John Nicholls died in 1621, that branch of the Nicholls family ceased to exist. There is little doubt that John Nicholls was the selfsame person who was licensed as a victualler by the Justices of the Peace.

At the time there was only one other Nicholls family in the town, that of Thomas Nicholls, which did not contain a John.

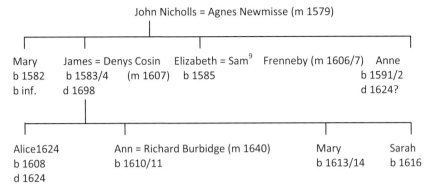

John Nicholls = Agnes Newmisse (m 1579)

Mary	James = Denys Cosin	Elizabeth = Sam[9] Frenneby (m 1606/7)	Anne
b 1582	b 1583/4 (m 1607) b 1585		b 1591/2
b inf.	d 1698		d 1624?

Alice1624	Ann = Richard Burbidge (m 1640)	Mary	Sarah
b 1608	b 1610/11	b 1613/14	b 1616
d 1624			

Perhaps we need one more piece of the jig-saw to prove the link between the ale house later known as the 'Prince Frederick's Head', John Nicholls himself, Nichol Lane, Thomas Simonds and the Burbridge family. However, we do know that Ann Nicholls, daughter of James and grand-daughter of John married a Burbridge; a Thomas Simonds owned the ale house in 1761 when a Henry Burbridge was the occupier, a Thomas Simonds owned the land and a building on it as early as 1723 and a Thomas Simonds of Plaistow had a daughter Ann in 1675. So after all that, although we cannot yet say beyond doubt that John Nicholls gave his name to the lane and the ale, we can certainly say that the odds are very short indeed.

Recent managers of the pub have included Faycol Fraj, Louise Betts, Michael Hullet, Niklas Farrow and Kate Lawrence.

The Prince Frederick survives despite a fire on the first floor when its classic opaque glass panelled ceiling in the bars below remained intact. To this day there is believed to be no other pub in the country named after 'Poor Fred'

Fig. 17 The Prince Frederick (1982)   *Photo: Stephen Goad*

---

[9] From records held in Bromley Central Library.

Plaistow Brewery

Legend has it, amongst the older residents of the area, that a brewery used to exist in Hollow Bottom. In fact, there is a great deal more to it than legend; there is no doubt of its existence. Plaistow Brewery was situated opposite the 'Prince Frederick' where Sheppey House now stands in Nichol Lane. The original building was occupied in 1841 by Thomas Gander, then aged 30, his wife and three children. His trade was that of a mealman. By 1861 Ezekiel Kelsey had moved into Hollow Bottom and by that time the business was definitely a brewery.

In 1852 Thomas Gander, by a deed of conveyance,[10] transferred ownership of the 'messuage, brewery and land in Hollow Bottom' to Ezekiel Kelsey. The transfer price was £500 of which £400 was granted as a mortgage by William Smith, of Deptford. At that time Thomas Gander, then aged 41, was out of business and living in Clapham. The previous transfer took place in 1839 when the property was made over to Thomas Gander by William Holland and his wife Ann. The list of items sold to Ezekiel Kelsey included two spring carts and a spring van, weighing machines, hogsheads, barrels and a complete range of brewing equipment. William Smith died in 1863 without having had the mortgage redeemed and the brewery was transferred by Gay Shute and others in 1871 into the possession of Henry Chamberlain with funds provided by Ellen Shuttleworth, widow of William Sewel Shuttleworth of Plaistow Hall. It is believed that she died in 1882.

The brewery was eventually converted into two cottages. Lucy Ann Shuttleworth, daughter of Ellen, swore an affidavit[11] in 1920, saying that she had for many years been familiar with the property known as Plaistow Brewery, owned by her mother, and that 'many years ago' it was converted into two cottages. A further cottage had been erected by her mother; the three being known as 20, 2l and 22 Nichol Lane. It therefore seems a safe assumption that the brewery closed in the 1880s or 1890s.

The 21st century population of Hollow Bottom may not know that it used to be the subject of a sort of social apartheid. There was a high wall across the end of Nichol Lane which segregated the worthy occupants of the two-up, two-downs from the polite society of Minster Road.

---

[10] From records held in Bromley Central Library
[11] From records held in Bromley Central Library

4

St Mary's Plaistow and the beginnings of St Andrew's

Events leading to consecration of St Andrew's Church, Bromley

1875	Iron Mission Room at Plaistow Lodge set high above Burnt Ash Lane (on London Lane side) run as a Chapel by Wm Hicks.
1888	Iron Mission Room in Farwig Lane - opposite Mooreland Road from 1888.
1896	St Mary's Church Institute, Plaistow Grove (by Queens Cottages) built for £300 by Wm Crossley
1903	Archbishop's Commission on Church Accommodation in Bromley decided that a new church beyond Plaistow Cemetery would meet all future requirements.
1905 (February)	Bishop of Croydon opened new St Mary's Hall in Farwig Hall in Farwig Lane.
1905	Lease on Mission Room in Farwig Lane expired. Institute in Plaistow Grove given over entirely to mission work. All other activities transferred to new church hall.
1905	St Mary's parish transferred from Diocese of Canterbury to Diocese of Rochester.
1907	Bishop of Rochester's Commission endorsed Archbishop's Commission report of 1903.
1907 (May 27th)	St Andrew's Mission Church in Nichol Lane dedicated for public worship (on site of Hadlow's Garage).
1908	St Mary's Institute closed and converted to three dwellings (now Nos. 43,43A and 43B Plaistow Grove).
1912	Sir Samuel Scott gave land opposite present St Andrew's Church.
1913	Iron Mission Church moved from site in Nichol Lane to new site opposite present Church.
1917	St Andrew's Mission Church temporarily closed.
1920 (Easter)	St Andrew's Mission Church re-opened.
1927 (Feb 7th)	Ecclesiastical Parish of St Andrew's, Bromley granted by Order in Council.
1927 (Mar. 24th)	Rev. J M T Griffiths licensed as first vicar.
1929	Work on new church began.
1929 (July 27th)	Foundation stone laid.
1930 (May 10th)	St Andrew's Church consecrated.

The origins of St Andrew's as an ecclesiastical parish are firmly rooted in the neighbouring parish of St Mary's, Plaistow. Thus we must go back to the 1860s to see how the church expanded to the north of Bromley.

Horsburgh[12] says

'The claims of the northern portion of the town were becoming insistent and about the year 1860 a scheme was set on foot to provide a church which should meet the wants of the district. Thus, largely through the liberal contributions of the Rev. H C Adams, Chaplain of the College (Bromley College), and his family, there came into existence the Church of St Mary, Plaistow, the nave being consecrated by Archbishop Longley in 1863. Since then the church has been enlarged by the additions of a south transept (1893) and a north transept, accompanied by a considerable extension of the vestries, (1900). A tower, however, is still lacking.

'Within, St Mary's owes much to the munificence of benefactors. The glass, by Mr Curtiss, of Ward and Hughes, is good, consisting of an east window erected by Lady Scott in memory of her husband, Sir Edward H Scott, a great benefactor of the church; two chancel windows commemorate two infant daughters of Major Clement Satterthwaite, who, for over forty years, was constant in his devotion towards the church; the seven windows in the nave are in memory of Mr Emmett, and six, also in the nave, given by Mr Murray Richardson, commemorate various members of his family. To Mr Murray Richardson also, the church owes its reredos and the decorations of the chancel.'

The area of Plaistow and Farwig in the 1860s was still rural as can be seen on the Ordnance Survey map for 1863 (Fig. 18) The part of College Road between Farwig Lane and London Lane was still known as Plaistow Lane. Cambridge Road, Crescent Road and Alma Grove (later part of Lansdowne Road) had come into existence, although no houses had yet been built there.

To the north of the parish were Plaistow Lodge, Plaistow Hall and Springhill whilst in Hollow Bottom a small group of cottages clustered around the 'Prince Frederick'

---

[12] *Bromley, Kent from the Earliest Times to the Present Century* by E L S Horsburgh (1929).

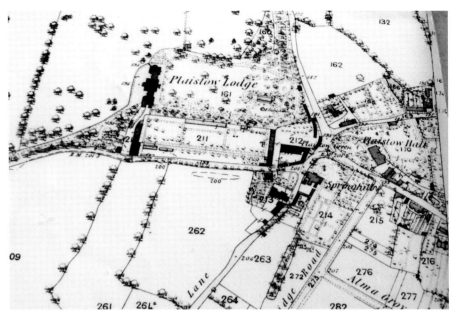

Fig. 18 Ordnance Survey Map 1863 showing Plaistow Lodge, Plaistow Hall, Springhill and the location of Hollow Bottom   *Courtesy: Bromley Central Library*

Horsburgh, writing of the 1860s says:

'To the north of the town there was open country beyond the College and from College Field (that is, from what is now the southern end of College Road) an uninterrupted view, extending to the church in the distance, could be obtained of stiles and meadows, shrubs and trees. '

Horsburgh plainly referred to St Mary's, Plaistow. No road existed between the Farwig Lane - College Road junction and the Market Square. There was a network of footpaths giving access to the National Schools practically from Farwig and other directions.

The emergence of St Andrew's as an ecclesiastical parish and as a church is traced through a series of mission rooms in the parish of St Mary's. An iron mission room stood in Farwig Lane almost opposite Mooreland Road from 1888. But thirteen years earlier, in 1875, *Strong's Directory of Bromley* first mentions the presence of a mission room adjacent to Plaistow Lodge Farm. In 1886 it is formally recorded in the same directory as a place of worship. This mission was almost certainly on the bend in the road where London Lane meets Burnt Ash Lane opposite the builder's yard (in 2012, the doctor's surgery).

It was here that the young William Hicks, son of the lessee of Plaistow Hall (across the road in Plaistow Lane), ran the mission. In 1896 St Mary's Church

Institute was built for £300 in Plaistow Grove by William Crossley. The land, which had previously been tennis courts, was presented by Sir Samuel Scott. The mission came under the guiding hand of Mr H P Steer who died in 1955.

The Rev. Angus MacFarlane[13] records that in 1900, at the Institute, there is mention of services which a robed choir and the hope had been expressed that the

Fig. 19 Mission Church at the top of Burnt Ash Lane, near Plaistow Green
Courtesy: Bromley Central Library;   *Photo restored by Lucy Gahagan*

building might be licensed for Holy Communion services. A year later funds were sufficient for the purchase of an American organ in place of the harmonium. At that time the choir consisted of thirteen boys, seven men and seven girls. In May 1903 the Rev. M C Wells was in charge of the Institute before leaving to become Vicar of Sittingbourne.

St Mary's vicar referred in 1903 to the moving of the iron mission room from Farwig Lane to a site at the top of Burnt Ash Lane to serve the growing district of Burnt Ash. This move was accomplished four years later. In his last parochial address (he left in 1904) the Rev. Bond stated that there were now 7,000 in the parish and at Easter he would ask for an additional curate. He announced that Sir Samuel Scott, on certain conditions, had promised to give a site, free of cost, nearly opposite the entrance to Plaistow Cemetery. The financial prospect demanded the raising of nearly £8,000, and he put forward a suggestion whereby, if the 200 householders laid by £5 10s per annum to be put on deposit, in five years the target would be reached.

---

[13] *St Mary's First Hundred Years 1863-1963*

The eventual urban development of the rural area north of St Mary's must have been clearly foreseen as the Archbishop's Commission on church accommodation in Bromley decided in 1903 that a new church beyond Plaistow Cemetery would meet all future requirements. The Institute in Plaistow Grove was still in existence in 1904, and it was there on October 7th that the departing vicar was presented with a bookcase and a cheque for £35, together with a silver paper knife from the boys at Quernmore School who attended his Bible class.

St Mary's built a new church hall in Farwig Lane which was opened by the Bishop of Croydon in 1905 in the presence of the former vicar, Mr Bond. The lease on the mission room in Farwig Lane expired in 1905 and the institute in Plaistow Grove was given over entirely to mission work, all other activities being transferred to the new hall.

It was then proposed that the other recommendations of the Archbishop of Canterbury's Commission should be carried out, and that the Institute should be abandoned and an iron mission room erected. This was achieved by Sir Samuel Scott substituting a new site in Nichol Lane for the existing one. The vicar stared that 'a committee had been formed of which the Rev. C de Wall is chairman, Col Robinson Hon. Treasurer and Mr Ernest Cawston Hon. Secretary, which committee is undertaking the erection of the building and the working up of the new district in view of the future church which will (as soon as this part of the parish is sufficiently developed) be erected beyond Plaistow Cemetery'.

Also in 1905 the parish of St Mary's was transferred from the Diocese of Canterbury to the Diocese of Rochester. Two years later the Bishop of Rochester's Commission endorsed the Archbishop's Commission report of 1903.

On 13th April 1907 Sir Samuel Scott Bart M P leased a site on the junction of Nichol Lane and Plaistow Lane to the then vicar of St Mary's, Rev. Edward Colebrooke, for five years at a rent of £1 per year, for the purpose of erecting a Mission Room.

On 27th May 1907 St Andrew's Mission Church was dedicated for public worship at a service conducted by Archdeacon Scott, vicar of St James', Tunbridge Wells.

It seated 200 people and Miss Bullen was the organist. A Bromley directory gives an impressive list of services, with Holy Communion at 6, 7, and 8am on Greater Festivals. Fig. 21 shows the robed choir of the Mission Church in a photograph taken between 1907 and 1909. This picture can be dated with a fair degree of precision as it is known that Mr Ted Munday, one of those pictured, moved from St Andrew's to St Mary's choir in 1911, and the curate, Mr de Wall left in 1909. As the mission church itself did not open until 1907 the photograph was taken between 1907/09. It shows us members of the Muncey family which must have been one of the largest families ever connected with St Andrew's.

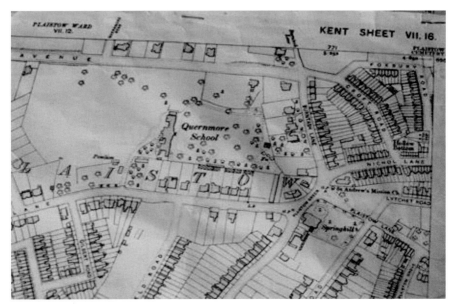

Fig. 20 Ordnance Survey 1:2500 map 1912 showing St Andrew's Mission Church on the junction of Burnt Ash Lane and Plaistow Lane   *Courtesy: Bromley Central Library*

Fig. 21 Choir of St Andrew's Mission Church, Plaistow Green c 1908

(L-R)   *Courtesy: Mrs E. Rose Muncey*

Back Row: 2nd Frank Muncey, 4th Tom Stone, 5th Charlie Muncey, 6th Mr Wright, 7th Ted Munday
Middle Row: 1st Herbert Muncey, 6th Mr Reeve(s?), 6th A Harden, 10th Mr Hughesman
Front Row: 3rd Arthur Muncey, 6th Rev C de Wall, 7th Mr Gibbs, 13th J Nettlingham

Those shown are Frank, Charlie, Arthur and Herbert. The last named together with the eldest brother William, cousin Harry and their uncle Henry all died during the Great War and their names appear on the wayside shrine above the font in St Andrew's Church. The family, who lived in Croft Road, comprised ten children in all. Of the five daughters, in 1982 three still lived in Crescent Road.

In 1908 the Institute in Plaistow Grove, which was considered to be poorly placed to cope with the needs of the developing part of St Mary's parish, was closed and converted into three houses within the one detached building. They survive as Nos. 43, 43A and 43B Plaistow Grove. Then in 1912 the Bishop of Rochester presided over a meeting of St Mary's parishioners, as a result of which Sir Samuel Scott made available land opposite the present St Andrew's Church to which the iron mission church building was moved from Nichol Lane. The minutes of the Easter Vestry meeting of St Mary's Plaistow, of 9th April, 1912 record 'moved by Mr Quelch, seconded by Mr Gumbrill and resolved, "That a special application be made to the police of this district to protect the congregation of St Andrew's from the brick and stone throwing at the Church which so frequently occur during services on Sunday and during choir practice." At the St Mary's Easter Vestry meeting of 15th April 1916 it was recorded that 'The accounts of the Mission Church of St Andrew's were presented and found to be satisfactory, there being a small balance in hand. It was the first time in its history that the Mission Church had been self-supporting.'

The origin of the name of Rangefield Road is interesting. According to Horsburgh Infantry volunteers were called for in 1849 as a repercussion of the Crimean War. Bromley answered the appeal of the Lord-Lieutenant of the day, Viscount Sydney, of Frognal, Chislehurst, and as a result the Rifle Corps, afterwards known as the 18th Kent, was formed. This eventually became the 2nd V B The Queen's Own Royal West Kent Regiment, which was in turn the parent of the 5th Bn Royal West Kents and the 20th Bn London Regiment of the Territorial Army. The Drill Hall in East Street was built in 1872.

Efficiency and marksmanship were essential and a rifle range on the Chin Brook between Grove Park and the Chislehurst Tunnel was opened in 1861, but it closed to permit building of the South Eastern main railway line via Chislehurst. A new range was located at Southend from which Rangefield Road on the Downham Estate gets its name. The Satterthwaites were active in the corps and both Major Clement and Colonel Edward Satterthwaite in turn commanded the corps.

Incidentally Butts Road, behind Rangefield School (which must surely claim the prize for the shortest street in the country) is connected with the range as this must have been the area where the targets were placed.

5

The Great War

Because almost all the congregation had volunteered for active service, attendance at the Mission Church had dropped away to an average of 15 to 20 people and with the Bishop's permission it was closed in 1917 to be re-opened three years later.

The names of those who fell during the Great War are commemorated on the wayside shrine now permanently placed at the west end of the church.

Fig. 22 Wayside Shrine above the font in St. Andrew's Church

Photo: Andrew Martin

For clarity they are:

John West Arnold.	RWK	William Edward Jenkins	12th Lon.Terrs
William Edwin Bagwell	1st Rifle BGDE	Percy John Leeds	RE
Bertram John Bagwell	RWK	L W Mallholie	
Frederick Edward Baker	RE	Percy William Meopham	RWK
George William Barnard	Gloucs.	Archibald Robert Moore	East. Lancs
Arthur James Edmund Brentnall	44th Aus.Inf	Herbert Muncey	RWK
Arthur Oliver Brickstock	RAMC	Henry James Muncey	RWK
Frederick William Brickstock	RAMC	William Muncey	Essex
Ernest Brown	RWK	Thomas Marcus Naylor	RN
William Owen Clarke	R Fus.	William George Newton	RN
Richard Collett		Henry William Page	RN
Reginald Luke Welfare Curtis	Coldstream Guards	James Herbert Porter	RFA
Thomas Ralph Dennis	RWK	Herbert Potter	RMLI
Sidney Leonard Eastwood	Surrey	Arthur Leslie Richards	RWK
Walter William Eastwood	R W Surrey	George Richards	Xth Canadians
Ernest Fairweather	Lon. Field Ambul	Edward Scutt	18th Australian Regt
William Albert Fry	Grenadier Guards	George Shelley	RE Surrey
Ernest Arthur Godward	RN	Leith Warlow	
Edward Gosling	R Fus.	Cecil Henry Winfield	R Fus.
Alfred Haffenden	RFA	James Percy Winfield	RWK
W. J. Harding	20th Lon. Terr	William Winterman	R Sussex

Bearing in mind that the ecclesiastical parish of St Andrew's was not created until 1927, the names are linked to both St Mary's parish and the emerging St Andrew's district. The following detailed information is sourced from Forces-War-Records, Commonwealth War Graves Commission records and elsewhere.

Pte John West Arnold aged 41, husband of Alice Arnold, of 2nd Bn Queen's Own Royal West Kent Regiment, died on 17th March 1915. His parents lived in Homesdale Road, Bromley. John Arnold was born in 1876 and was a builder's carman, lived in Page Heath Villas, was married to Alice Elizabeth Arnold and left three children, Bessie Dorothy, James West and John Alfred.

Pte Bertram John Bagwell, aged 20, died on 16th July 1918. He was attached to 8th Bn, QORWK Regt. His parents Mr & Mrs J E Bagwell lived at 34, Lansdowne Rd, Bromley. His name appears on the Memorial at Bully-Grenay Communal Cemetery, British Extension, 15km north of Arras, Pas de Calais, France. Bertram was the brother of William Edwin, born in 1898. He is commemorated on the family head-stone at Plaistow Cemetery, noted as interred in France.

William Edwin Bagwell Signaller 1st Bn Rifle Brigade died aged 25 on 17th August 1918. He was born in 1894 and was a railway clerk living (in 1911) at 8 Weston Road, Bromley with his parents, John Edwin and Emma, and sister Maud Elizabeth. It appears that they moved to Lansdowne Road after 1911. He is also commemorated on the same Bagwell family headstone. Thus the family lost its two sons within a month of each other. Their father John Edwin died in his 67th year in 1925 and his widow Emma lived to the age of 91 and died in 1954.

Spr F E Baker, of the Royal Engineers Regt died on 1st December 1918. He is commemorated at Plaistow Cemetery, Bromley (Grave G 'C' 39). A Frederick Edward Baker is recorded on ancestry.com at Brightlingsea, Essex on 1st December 1918, and there is a family tree on Ancestry which would suggest that he was the brother of Marian Daisy. He was baptised along with brother Albert George at St Mary's Church, Princes Road, Lambeth in 1882, address 14, Cardigan Street. His birth was registered in 1878. In 1899 he married Mary Ann and in 1901 lived in Esher Street, Lambeth and worked in marble and they had a 1 year old daughter Elsie.

L/Cpl G W Barnard, of the 1st Bn, Gloucestershire Regt died on 16th March 1915. He is commemorated at Plaistow Cemetery, Burnt Ash Lane, Bromley. George William Barnard was born in 1882 in Bromley and was married to Julie Gertrude with a daughter Kathleen May (born 1910); they lived at 17 Moorelands Road, Bromley in 1911; he was a plumber

Pte James Brentnall, aged about 25, died of wounds on 17th October 1918. He was born at Normanby, Yorkshire and served in the 44th Bn, Australian Infantry, Service No. 3610. Arthur James Edmund Brentnall's parents were Arthur Street Brentnall and Annie Maria Brentnall. He was a motor engineer and that he lived at 66 Nichol Lane. He is commemorated at Plaistow Cemetery, (Grave 3610/L84).

Arthur Oliver Brickstock was born in Godmanchester, Huntingdonshire in about 1889 and was a private in the Welsh Regiment in Egypt in 1911; his parents were Frederick and Fanny, and siblings were Frederick, George and Edith, in 1901 living in Perry Hill, Lewisham. **Frederick William Brickstock** was also born in Godmanchester in 1884, son of Frederick and Fanny. In 1911 he was living at 21, Croft Road, Bromley, an assistant draper.

Ernest Brown. There was a Pte E J Brown of QORWK Regt who died, aged 26, on 24th July 1915 and who is commemorated at the Basra War Cemetery (Grave/Memorial II R 8). His parents were Annie Edwards (formerly Brown) of 40, North Street, St Peter's, Tunbridge Wells who was born in Crowborough, Sussex.

There was an Ernest Brown born in Bromley in about 1891, son of the widowed George Brown, and lived at 40 Martins Road, occupation: a domestic gardener. However there was also a William Ernest Brown who was born at Needham Market, Suffolk in about 1879, son of Cornelius and Isabella Brown, Cornelius being a carpenter. In 1911 William Ernest was living at 44, Simpsons Road, Bromley with his wife Hariett Amy, William being a porter in an ironmongers. CWGC records show that Pte William Ernest Brown, Service No., 1138 of the 5th Bn QORWK Regt died on 14th May 1915, is buried at Jhansi Cantonment Cemetery, India and is commemorated in name only on the Madras 1914-1918 War Memorial, Chennai, Face 20. H died on the same day as Henry James Muncey (see below).

William Owen Clarke is something of a mystery; the only person of this name in 1911 was 1 year old; accurately finding a William Clarke is difficult and the only guess is one born in 1878 in Harmondon, Kent, living with his mother and sister at 9 Vale Cottages, Masons Hill in 1911, a labourer/builder by trade.

Richard Collett: the only person who seems to be possible would have been very young, even at the end of the conflict, being born in 1902. Parents Charles and Lilian, born in Herne Hill, and living with numerous siblings at 3, Blyth Road, Bromley in 1911.

Pte Reginald Curtis, serving with the Coldstream Guards died on 31st January 1915. Reginald Curtis (without the middle names) was born in Wroughton, Wiltshire, in 1889, and in 1911 lived with his parents at 38, Nichol Lane, his occupation being ex-soldier.

Pte Thomas Dennis of 2nd/4th Bn QORWK Regt, aged 18, died on 19th October 1915. His mother was Mrs C Dennis of 54, Nichol Lane, Bromley. 2nd/4th Bn landed at Suvia Bay, Gallipoli on 10th August 1915 and was evacuated from Gallipoli on 13th December 1915 and moved to Egypt.

L/Cpl Sidney Eastwood , with 8th Bn Queen's Royal West Surrey Regt. Died on 12th August 1916 at the age of 19. His parents were Henry and Ellen Eastwood of 29 Nichol Lane, Bromley. Three months later his brother **L/Cpl Walter Eastwood**, aged 26, of 1st Bn of the same regiment met his death on 12th August 1916.

Pte Ernest Fairweather, aged 21, of 2nd/1st London Field Ambulance (RAMC,) died on 24th September 1916. His parents were John and Mary Emma Fairweather, 4, Plaistow Grove, Bromley.

Pte William Fry, of 3rd Bn, Grenadier Guards was killed on 15th September 1916. The Battalion, formed at Wellington Barracks, London landed at Le Havre on 27th July 1915 and came under the command of 2nd Guards Brigade, Guards Division in 19th August that year.

Ernest Arthur Godward was born in 1898 in Eastbourne and in 1911 was living with his step-parents, John and Theresa Lane at 35, Foxbury Road, Bromley. He is commemorated at Plaistow Cemetery with the words 'My Dear Boy, Ernest Arthur Godward R E who died August 31st 1920, He fought the good fight'. On the wayside shrine his name is given as Ernest Arthur Godward R N. However on the grave-stone his service is R E not R N. Ernest would only have been about 19 when the war ended.

L/Cpl Edward Gosling, of 4th Bn Royal Fusiliers (London Regt) died on 22nd July 1916.

Driver Alfred Haffenden, aged 33, of Royal Field Artillery died on 22nd October 1914. He was the husband of E A Haffenden of 10, Albert Road, Bromley. Alfred Haffenden's wife's name was Elizabeth; born in Eastbourne, had a son Alfred born in 1905.

W J Harding: It is difficult to verify without a forename, but likely to be William Leslie born in Bromley in 1898, son of W and A Harding living at 20, Hilldrop Road.

William Edward Jenkins: No information found other than a William Henry Jenkins who lived at 41, Croft Rd., Bromley immediately before the war.

Percy John Leeds was born in 1883 and married to Harriett Cooper Leeds with a daughter, Doris Mary, born 1910. He was born in Gravesend and was a sorting clerk/telegraphist, and they lived at 40, Croft Road.

L W Mallholie appears to be a transcription error as there appears to be no relevant information either in military records or in the 1911 census.

Pte P Mepham who died on Christmas Day, Dec 25th 1916 is commemorated at Plaistow Cemetery, Bromley (Grave C27). This must surely be the Percy William Meopham QORWK whose name appears on the wayside shrine at St Andrew's. His name was shown in 1911 as Mepham (as signed by his father) and as shown by his birth and lived at 21, Gladwell Road, son of William and Mary Ann; Percy was born 1894 and was a draper porter. He had a sister Gladys Mary and a brother Harold George. Pte Mepham's name appears on Grave/Memorial C27 at Plaistow Cemetery, Bromley. Meopham is of course a village in Kent which would possibly explain the spelling on the wayside shrine.

Sgt Archibald Robert Moore, aged 26, of the East Lancashire Rgt died on 6th April 1915. He was born in Cape Town, S. Africa and was the son of Mrs Agnes Moore of 29, Ker Street, Devonport and the late Robert Moore.

Pte Henry James Muncey, of 5th Bn QORWK Regt died on 14th May 1915. 1/5th Bn was a Territorial Bn formed at the Drill Hall, East Street, Bromley in August 1914. They became a Brigade, Home Counties Division. By 30th October 1914 they had moved to India. On arrival in Bombay the Division was broken up and transferred to the Jhansi Brigade, 5th (Mhow) Division, Indian Army. Capt. C.T. Atkinson's *The Queen's Own Royal West Kent Regiment 1914-1919* records that both 1/4th and 1/5th Battalions lost a number of men through sickness. According to military records he is buried at Jhansi (Lynchgate) Cantonment Cemetery in Jhansi. This cemetery which had fallen into disrepair was restored largely due to the determined activities of 88-year old Mrs M R (Peggy) Cantern, who after her husband's death in 1986 changed her plans to repatriate to UK and stayed to work in the local community.

Strangely there is no gravestone with Henry Muncey's name, but there are several unreadable. According to CWGC records Henry James Muncey's name does appear on the Madras 1914-1918 War Memorial, in Chennai (formerly Madras) on Face 20. The memorial bears the names of more than 1,000 servicemen who died during the Great War, who lie in many civil and cantonment cemeteries in various parts of India.

The only person named Henry James Muncey was born in 1864 which would make him 50 or 51 at the time of his death in 1915. This clearly means that he was a generation older than the great majority of those who lost their lives during the Great War. He was born in Blackheath, married to Alexandra and living with daughters Elizabeth, Beatrice and May Agnes at 51, Foxbury Road, Bromley, and he was uncle to William and Herbert who also perished in the war.

Henry James Muncey *died on the self-same day and at the same place at Jhansi, India as William Ernest Brown*. The two were members of the same battalion (5th) of the same regiment (Queen's Own, Royal West Kents). It therefore appears that these two were comrades in arms who could well have volunteered together and travelled together to India and died on the same day.

Henry Muncey died of heart failure. A significant number of men are known to have died of heat-stroke in India. In Northern India in May the temperature can reach very high levels and Henry Muncey was not in the first flush of youth. The MO reporting the circumstances of his death which occurred at about 4 p.m. recorded that the shade temperatures on the day he died ranged from a minimum of 89deg F (32deg C) to a maximum of 114deg F (over 45deg C). Aside from Capt Cooper (see page 49/50) 10 servicemen died during May and June 1915 at Jhansi.

It is remarkable that Henry had volunteered originally for one year's embodied service at home as a member of the Territorial Force, the 5th Bn Royal West Kent Regt on 5th August 1914 at the relatively advanced age of 50. He only served for two months before being posted to India. Only nine months later he was dead. Subjecting himself to the rigours of sub-tropical India at the height of the hot season must have taken considerable courage.

Henry James Muncey was the father of three daughters but had no sons. His occupation was that of a gardener.

Pte William Ernest Muncey, aged 26 of the 2nd Bn, Royal Sussex Regt (shown on the shrine as 'Essex') who died on 9th September 1916, son of Ernest Muncey of 11, Croft Rd, Bromley, husband of Clara Ada Muncey of 44, Liddon Rd, Bromley.

William was Henry's nephew as was the third member of the family to lose his life in the Great War

Cpl Herbert Henry Muncey of 6th Bn QORWK Regt who died on 3rd May 1917. Herbert Muncey was born in Bromley in 1896 and lived with his parents, Ernest and Ellen at 11, Croft Road in 1911 together with siblings William Ernest, Frank George, Charles Edward, Arthur Thomas, Winnie, Gladys and Rose (daughters only get one name!). Herbert is commemorated at Arras Memorial, France, Bay 7.

Thomas Marcus Naylor appears to have been born in Greenwich in 1887; there is a record of the death of Thomas M Naylor in Bromley in 1919.

William George Newton: No relevant information found.

Henry William Page: Leading Seaman H W Page RN attached to HMS Llewellyn died on 23rd October 1916. There was a Henry Page, labourer, born 1875 in Battersea, living at 23, Plymouth Road, Bromley in 1911 with his wife, Sarah, children Emma, Dorothy, Reginald, Bernard and Claude.

Dvr James Herbert Porter with Royal Field Artillery died at sea on the 23rd October 1915. He came from Hildenborough but enlisted in Bromley; There is a birth in 1880 of James Herbert Porter in Sevenoaks which would fit with Hildenborough. The information on Ancestry is that he died on the SS Marquette, near Greece, and married Mabel Grace Seal, born Bromley in 1881, in 1907 in Pontypridd. In 1911 he was working as a haulier below ground in a colliery in Wales. His birthplace was Leigh in Kent.

Pte Herbert Potter, aged 38, of the Royal Marines Light Infantry died on 3rd February 1915. He was the son of John Potter, husband of Frances Amelia Potter of 52, Nichol Lane, Bromley.

Pte Arthur Leslie Richards, aged 21, of A Company, 1st Bn QORWK Regt died on 1st June 1916. Arthur was a brother of George.

Pte George Richards, aged 25, of 10th Bn Canadian Infantry (Alberta Regt) died on 24th May 1915. His parents were George William and Fanny Richards of Llantrithyd, Cowbridge, Glam., Wales. Arthur Leslie Richards was born in Bridgend, Glamorganshire in 1896 and lived at 43, Nichol Lane, Bromley. His parents were George William and Fanny, and his siblings were Elizabeth, Harold Francis and Violet. In 1911 he was a groundsman on a golf course. The 1911 census states that George was born in Tatsfield, Surrey and Fanny was born in Wotton under Edge, Gloucestershire. At that time their address was 43, Nichol Lane.

Pte Charles Edward Scutt, aged 26 of 18th Bn, Australian Infantry died on 14th May 1916. His parents were Warden Scutt and Florence Ann Scutt, of 14, Park End, Bromley. Charles Edward Scutt was born in Bromley in 1890. In 1891 he was living at 14, Park End with his parents and siblings William, Harry, Florence and Emily; in 1901 they were still at the same address with the addition of Robert and Helen.

Pte George Shelley, aged 20, of 8th Bn, East Surrey Regt died on 23rd March 1918. He was the son of Ernest and Annie Shelley of 52, Lansdowne Rd, Bromley.

Lieut. Edmund Jarvis Leith Warlow, aged 22, of 11th Bn attached to 2nd Bn Worcestershire Regt died on 6th November 1916. His parents were the Ven. Archdeacon Edmund John Warlow MA and the late Emily Rose Warlow (née Hunter-Adam). In 1901 Leith Warlow lived at 32, Hammelton Road, Bromley with his parents, brother Cecil and sister Mary.

Pte Cecil Henry Winfield, aged 20, with 7th Bn Royal Fusiliers (London Regt) died on 23rd April 1917. His parents were James and Jessie Winfield of 65, Nichol Lane, Bromley. The 7th Bn had disembarked at Le Havre 24th Jul 1916. Cecil Henry Winfield had been a milkman.

The name of **Pte P J Winfield** of 7th Bn QORWK Regt who died on July 19th 1916 appears on a head-stone at Plaistow Cemetery, Bromley (Grave /Memorial K 83). James Percy Winfield, brother of Cecil Henry also worked in the dairy. They had a sister, Gladys Jessie.

Pte William R Winterman, aged 28, of 16th (Sussex Yeomanry) Bn, Royal Sussex Regt died on 21st September 1918. According to military records he was husband to Everelda White (formerly Winterman)* of 2, Wakering Ave., Shoeburyness, Essex. William Robert Winterman born 1886 lived at 19, Croft Road, Bromley in 1911 with his parents, Henry James and Sarah Ann and his brothers Henry James and Stanley ; he was a groom. * This could be a transcription error; her maiden name may have been White.

Yet Another Muncey perished in the war, who does not feature on the wayside shrine. He was **Cpl Harry Muncey** of the 13th Bn Royal Fusiliers who died aged 25 on 10th July 1916. He is buried at Etaples Military Cemetery. Harry's parents were William Stiddulph Muncey and Martha Muncey of Bromley. William Stiddulph was the brother of Ernest Stiddulph Muncey (who lost two sons) and Henry (Harry) James Muncey who also died. In 1911 Harry had been living with his parents at 8, Weston Grove, Bromley and was a surveyor's clerk. Few families can have suffered the loss of so many family members; three between the ages of 21 and 26 and their uncle.

The names of a number of World War I casualties appear on head-stones at Plaistow Cemetery, Burnt Ash Lane, Bromley.

Those so commemorated are as follows:

Name	Service Number	Date of Death	Age	Regiment / Service	Grave/ Memorial Service
Pte Alder, G E	7689	31/05/1921	27	2nd Dragoons (Royal Scots Greys)	S. 52.
Spr Baker, F E	184061	01/12/1918		Royal Engineers	G. "C" 39.
Lieut Bedford-Pim, Edward Woodley		05/07/1918	23	Royal Field Artillery	B. 8 and 20.
Pte Blackburn, R C	201823	27/11/1919		Queen's Own (Royal West Kent Regiment)	L. 79.
Pte Boorman, Leonard Richard	59091	24/10/1919	23	Bedfordshire Regiment	H. "C." 48.
Pte Brentnall, James	3610	17/10/1918	25	Australian Infantry, A.I.F.	L. 84.
Rfn Brookes, George	2104	28/09/1914	34	King's Royal Rifle Corps	C.General. 36.
Cpl Browne, Victor Arthur Lewis	930561	05/11/1918	29	Royal Field Artillery	L. 24.
Prob. FO Collett, N C		29/01/1918		Royal Naval Air Service	A. 95.
Gnr Dunk, A H	177366	14/09/1918	33	Royal Garrison Artillery	A. 144.
Col Griffith, Frank		04/01/1917	55	Royal Field Artillery	C. 29 and 38.
Pte Hills, P E	1094	07/06/1917		Royal Fusiliers	B. "C." 5.
L/Cpl Hone, G	P/3906	04/03/1918	41	Military Police Corps	F. 41.
Pte Kimber, Albert John	20113	05/01/1918	40	Queen's Own (Royal West Kent Regiment)	G. 54.
Air Mech, 2nd Cl Manning, H J	54269	15/02/1917		Royal Flying Corps	S. 48.
Pte Mepham, P W	G/1283	25/12/1916		Queen's Own (Royal West Kent Regiment)	C. 27.
2 L/T Trollope, Cyril Harvey		04/05/1917	20	Royal Flying Corps	L. 81.
Pte Tuffley, Frank	204014	08/05/1917	34	The Buffs (East Kent Regiment)	K. 73.
Stoker 1st Cl. Waters, David	SS/11376 3	15/04/1919		Royal Navy	G. 10.
Pte Winfield, P J	G/1289	19/07/1916		Queen's Own (Royal West Kent Regiment)	K. 83.
Lieut. Col Wright, W		13/05/1916		Army Service Corps	E. 1.

Note 1 This list may not be exhaustive.

2 Lt Trollope was accidentally killed while flying on 4th May 1917. He was the only child of John Basil and Effie Trollope.

We need to go to India to cover an area of the QORWK's history where we can pencil in some missing pieces of the jigsaw puzzle linked to Bromley.

In addition to those listed above the names of a number of World War I casualties appear on head-stones at Plaistow Cemetery, Burnt Ash Lane, Bromley who had strong links with the local area. It is highly unlikely that any military servicemen killed in action overseas or who died from any other cause would have been repatriated to UK, so the great majority of the names appearing on family grave-stones are clearly in memoriam to war dead.

Lieut Edward Woodley Bedford Pim, aged 23, Royal Field Artillery, died on 5th July 1918. His father, Henry Pim, born in 1863 in Hampstead was married to Mabel. In 1901 he was living at 7, Spencer Road, Plaistow, and was a Clerk in Holy Orders (a clergyman of the C of E). Edward was born in Newbury, Berkshire in the summer of 1894 as Edward Bedford Pim. They had a daughter as well as Edward, and three live-in servants. In 1911 Edward was at Wellington College public school in Berkshire. Their house in Plaistow was called 'Leaside'. Military records show that Edward's father was living at Upper Norwood, Surrey, so he may have moved there later.

Captain G.S. Cooper is recorded on the family head-stone as 'Killed in Jhansi, India June 28th 1915. Forces-war-records.co.uk records that he is buried at Jhansi Cantonment Cemetery, as is Henry Muncey. This is confirmed by CWGC. The dates of death for the two were only six weeks apart.

Capt. C.T. Atkinson's *The Queen's Own Royal West Kent Regiment 1914-1919* records that the 1/5th (as they were then styled) lost several men through sickness including Lieut Burr, who died on 6th May 1915. However the death of Capt. Cooper came differently. Two sepoys (or 'sowars') ran amok and murdered Capt. Cooper and two other British officers and an NCO. Regimental records show that the others killed on the date concerned (28th June 1915) were Lieut. Arthur Patrick Courtenay and Major Marmeduke H L Gale both of 8th Indian Cavalry and two other ranks lost their lives in the same incident. They were Pte Evan Edwards (3902287), 2nd Bn South Wales Borderers and Bmbr Charles John Cooper (72783) 79th Bty Royal Field Artillery, which is one more casualty that Atkinson records.

All these are commemorated in name only on the Madras 1914-1918 War Memorial, Chennai. The records show that the two 'sowars' were brothers. One had been instructed to proceed with a draft to the Front. The other wished to go too, but his wishes were not granted. Infuriated, they left their lines at 8 a.m. that morning and killed two officers of their own regiment, Major Gale, who was shot dead and Lieut Courtenay who died of gun-shot and sabre wounds, and shot and wounded Capt. Hudson their Adjutant. They made for the station staff office and en-route met a bombardier (Bmbr Charles John Cooper) and a sergeant of the RFA, shot dead the former and wounded the latter.

Unfortunately Capt. G S Cooper, who was acting as Station Staff Officer at the time, had just left the office and was on his way to breakfast when the two sowars arrived. They let Capt. Cooper pass, but as soon as he had done so they immediately shot him in the back. He died instantly. Shortly after this the two murderers were themselves shot dead when some artillery men turned out on hearing the sound of firing.

The regimental records state that they had lost a good regimental officer, a good sportsman and a thoroughly keen and very popular officer. All ranks mourned his loss. This means that at least three of those who perished at Jhansi and are buried at the Jhansi Cantonment Cemetery have strong connections with Bromley. Also recorded on the Plaistow Cemetery is evidence of another tragedy in the Cooper family; George and his wife Clara had lost their son Ronald Stanley in July 1912, who died prior to his second birthday, and Clara herself.

Fig. 23   Madras World War 1 Memorial (now Chennai) India
Courtesy: Commonwealth War Graves Commission

Figs. 24 Cooper memorial stones

Photos: Andrew Martin

Fig. 25 Bagwell memorial stone

Capt. George Stanley Cooper was born in Catford in 1881. His father was a letterpress printer, born in Hackney. His mother Mary was born in Littlehampton. In 1891 he was living at 11, Tweedy Road, Bromley with his parents, siblings and two servants; his occupation, like his father, was that of a printer. Ten years later in 1901 now aged about 20, he lived at 29, London Road, Bromley, with parents, four siblings a parlour-maid and cook (the cook was Alice M Church). His father was listed as a printer with his own business. In 1911, now aged about 30, he was at Highfield, Westmoreland Road, Bromley with his wife Clara, née Tilling, daughter Mary Clara born in 1907 in Bromley and son Ronald Stanley born in 1910/11. They were living with his wife's parents, Edward and Clare Tilling, plus a domestic nurse in a 10-bedroomed house. George was by that time a printer in his own business (probably having taken over the business from his father on retirement). He was then called to the flag and was tragically murdered at Jhansi, India.

Another casualty who does not appear on the wayside shrine is Rifleman Leonard Henry Bedford. On a grave-stone at Plaistow Cemetery are the words 'Missing in France October 1916 aged 21 years'. In forces-war-records.co.uk his service No. is recorded as S/15141 and was serving with the 1st Bn Rifle Brigade and died on 18th October 1916. His name is commemorated on the grave-stone of his mother Florence Emily Bedford who died in 1931 and Henry Bedford who died aged 82 in 1950. Rfmn Bedford is also commemorated in name only on the Thiepval Memorial, Somme, France, Pier and Face 16B and 16C. Military records use Harry as his second name. Like many thousands of World War 1 casualties he is buried 'somewhere in France'.

Little did the populace of Hollow Bottom, Burnt Ash and Sundridge Park know in 1919 that, having suffered such loss of life during the Great War, they would again be visited by death and destruction only 20 years or so later. This time it would be not only through the loss of many of those again called to military service, but through the destruction of their very homes during the Blitz.

Fig. 26 Alan Wells who tends the Plaistow Cemetery gardens in 2012 *Photo: Andrew Martin*

Fig. 27 The Drill Hall, at the centre of Bromley, has been converted into a congenial bar for O'Neill's.

Photo: Andrew Martin

The West Kents

And so
The young, and not so young
Men and boys of Bromley
Bright eyed, Full of hope
In the Drill Hall
Did their duty, Volunteered
And signed, on the line
For 'embodied service'
And joined the flood
Of millions
Who into battle rode
As if on horse-back
With that pernicious, clammy, black, eternal shadow
Death
Riding pillion

AJM Aug. 2012

6
The 1920s

At the time of the war, the mission was the responsibility of the vicar of St Mary's and was almost entirely left in the charge of the curates who succeeded each other during the long incumbency of the Rev. William Gowans. The late Bessie Bartholomew records that now and again the vicar himself would pay a visit to the mission and harangue the parishioners from the pulpit in his north-country accents.

In 1982 there were still several people who had clear recollections of attending the 'Tin Church'. Mrs Morris, widow of Bill Morris, would attend evensong with her friends Mrs Jarvis and Mrs Ridley.

Fig. 28   St Andrew's 'Tin Church' close to the present site of Waitrose
Courtesy of Mr L Burbridge

Fig. 29   Interior of St Andrew's 'Tin Church', Burnt Ash Lane
Photo: St Andrew's Church archives

Fig. 30 Reservoir: Powster's Hill   *Courtesy: Bromley Central Library*

The reservoir on top of Powster's Hill was constructed in 1922. This must have been a very considerable undertaking. Photos (Figs 30 & 31) show that a railhead was built to supply the materials including cement and aggregates for the concrete columns. The structure was roofed in with reinforced concrete, then the whole thing was covered and grassed and remains there nearly a century later. On one corner is a trig point (or triangulation point) used in the mapping of the country by Ordnance Survey.

Fig. 31 Reservoir: Powster's Hill   *Courtesy: Bromley Central Library*

Bessie Bartholomew in her *Short History of St Andrew's, Bromley,* (1951) recalled the parish as it was in those days.

'My earliest recollection of St Andrew's is of walking down to it from St Mary's. There were no Sunday Schools here in the early days and we attended St Mary's. Occasionally, on a summer morning, the whole school, instead of going into St Mary's for Mattins, took a country walk, down College Road and Burnt Ash Hill, across a field full of cows, and over the road to St Andrew's. The church (Fig. 28) was almost opposite the site of our present church and stood a little way back from the road among the fields, and was approached by a gravel path flanked with flowering currant bushes. Thirty years ago, the Mission Church, Sundridge Hall, and Sundridge Farm and its two cottages, were the only buildings on that side of the road between the present vicarage and the houses just this side of Grove Park Station, and the cottages either side of Gladwell and Hilldrop Roads and the cemetery gate house were the only buildings on the opposite side.

It is difficult to indicate the extent of the difference in the character of the district in the earlier days. The main thoroughfare, Burnt Ash Lane, has been completely altered. Then it was a lane indeed, narrow, twisting, pathless, and tree-lined most of its length from Croft Road to its junction with Baring Road. The unlovely dips and undulations in our church lawn reveal where once a row of elms stood. The section of lane between the church and Grove Park was very steep and narrow; it has since been straightened, widened, and decapitated out of recognition.

'Gladwell and Hilldrop Roads were confronted by the green slopes of Powster's Hill, which, according to local history, is thought to have been a British settlement in ancient days. It was noted as the only circular view-point in Bromley.

The picture (Fig. 32) from the late John Smith's archive (for which I am indebted to Steve Silverthorne and Ray Fowler) evokes the atmosphere of the sudden intrusion of urban development on the rural landscape less than a century ago.

"The view southwards from its heights is still good; then one could see the Thames to the north. It provided us with the joys, according to season, of tobogganing, blackberrying, tree-climbing, and fishing in the pond which lay on its summit before the huge reservoir was constructed. Annually, Sanger's circus, and sometimes a fair, pitched in one of the fields at its foot, and an amusing incident comes to mind. At the time of the Irish troubles a carload of Sinn Feiners was stopped by the police in the lane, and after one revolver shot they scattered and ran. Next day a revolver was found in a field bordering the lane, and every year afterwards circuses and fairs advertised that they were coming to the Battle Field, Burnt Ash Lane.

Fig. 32 Hilldrop Road, Bromley 1918
Photo from archives of the late John Malcolm Smith enhanced by Tony Isbitt Photography

'Brook Lane led to the brook, a winding stream making its own way across the meadows to Southend, with cows drinking at it and skylarks rising on every side; New Street Hill, then Mottingham Lane, was a beautiful country lane, hedged with high banks of hawthorn; and what are now the Downham and Ayling estates were open fields, with sheep and cattle grazing. Although nothing now remains of the pastoral scene, the knowledgeable eye can still trace the fields and hedges by means of such little landmarks as the old elm in front of the flats in Southover and the remnant of hawthorn hedge in Roslin Way.

'Even in those quiet days we had quite a good congregation at the little church. It was a reasonably spacious building; the altar, organ and choir-stalls were on a raised platform (the altar is now in the lady chapel of the present church and the stalls are in the choir vestry) and the tiny window over the altar was filled with stained glass. One organ we had was hand-pumped and the handle had to go through the wall into the vestry, which meant that the organist was one side of the wall and the organ blower the other, a rather Gilbertian situation which, however, seemed to work. My earliest recollections are of a lady organist, a Miss Burton, and a strict choirmaster, a Mr Hughesman, and the names of families who supplied the choirboys are still familiar ones here thirty years later - Bull, Durbin, Bartholomew and Bushby. 'Odd moments did occur. Some remember the hot Sunday evening when it was too stifling to hold the service inside and we carried our chairs out on to the seemingly innocent grass, only to find ourselves shortly afterwards kneeling on stinging nettles. My mother's entry to the 8 am service one morning was barred by a goat that stood in the porch and showed every intention of going in with her. It was removed by the caretaker, old Jack Bagwell, who was also verger and loudest singer in the choir. We children always waited with joyful anticipation his singular rendering of the high tenor notes in the last line of "Fight the good fight".

'With the building of houses in Burnt Ash Lane and Avondale Road, and the development of the LCC Downham Estate, our congregations grew, and on such occasions as harvest festivals the church was packed. More people will remember these days, the times of the Rev. Cuthbert Cooper; the Rev. M Parker Shipman, a kindly, somewhat eccentric man who always had a string of children literally hanging to his coattails as he paraded the parish, umbrella in hand; and the Rev. G E Parsons, last curate-in-charge of St Andrews.'

Between 1920 and 1925 there must have been considerable impetus to put the recommendations of the Archbishop's Commission into effect and in 1925 the antecedent of St Andrews Parochial Church Council came into existence. It was the St Andrew's Guild of Fellowship (not to be confused with St Andrew's Guild of Service which was formed in 1930).

The first Guild Meeting of Representatives of St Mary's Parochial Church Council was held at 58, Lansdowne Road on 29th December, 1925, to constitute the Guild and to appoint Officers and members of the Council and to adopt regulations for its management.

Fig. 33 Rev G E Parsons
Photo: St Andrew's archives

Rev. G E Parsons, was appointed Warden of the Guild and the officers were Mr and Mrs F H Sherriff, H Evers, C Sheldon and L S Manvell. The Guild drew up a set of rules and arrangements were made to cater for a wide range of church and social activities including the choir under the redoubtable Mr H G Woodhams and the Dramatic Society under Miss Lamb. Apart from church services on Sundays, the Mission Hall was used each weekday evening.

At one meeting it was reported that the verger, W J Aspinall, was not carrying out his duties in a satisfactory manner, and after discussion and serious deliberation it was resolved that the Deputy Wardens give him one month's notice to terminate his engagement as Verger and inform him that if during that period his work be performed in a manner entirely satisfactory to the Priest in Charge the Council would be prepared to reconsider its decision. Mr Aspinall evidently had no intention of mending his ways and handed in his keys on 8th January. Mrs Porter thereafter was appointed caretaker of the Mission Church until 30th April at a weekly wage of 12/-.

At the monthly Guild meeting held on 1st March 1926 attention was drawn to the meeting of Parishioners to be held at St Mary's Hall on 4th March to discuss the new church. Mr F H Sherriff was appointed to represent the St Andrew's district on the committee for raising the Endowment Fund for the new church (the Ecclesiastical parish did not at that time exist). The first quarterly meeting of the Guild of Fellowship was held on 24th March 1926. A complete list of those present is preserved in the archives

Rev. G E Parsons left on 28th November, 1926, and Rev. J Martin T Griffiths arrived at St Andrew's on 12th January 1927 and became the new Warden of the Guild. The Council of the Guild of Fellowship discussed social events, finance, formation of the new parish, visiting residents of the district, music and formation of youth organisations. At the Guild Meeting of 28th February 1927 Rev. Griffiths announced arrangements for the Bishop to attend on 24th March to license him. In March it was resolved that the Easter election of Officers and members of the new Parochial Church Council would take place on 27th April. There was then a gap of

Fig. 34   Rev. J M T Griffiths, the first vicar of St Andrew's
Photo: St Andrew's archives

several months before the ninth meeting on 17th November to pass a resolution to wind up the Guild, and this was put into effect at the final general meeting on 16th January, 1928.

1927 marked the building of Burnt Ash School. It opened with three departments: the Infant's School, a Boys' Elementary School and a Girls' elementary School. In 1949 the boys were transferred to Quernmore and the Junior School came into existence. Thus it remained for 18 years. Miss D Cannon, who had been headmistress of the Girls' school between 1954 and the time it closed in 1967, remained at the school, which in 1982 was used as the headquarters for probationary teachers in Bromley.

George Lloyd, much respected headmaster of Burnt Ash Junior Mixed School, retired in 1969 at the end of the Summer term after 20 years stewardship in the post. He was the first headmaster of the school and came to Burnt Ash via a spell with Lloyds of London followed by his London University degree and teaching posts in the Old Kent Road, Raglan Road School and the Parish School in College Road, Bromley.

Sundridge Park Working Men's Club stands in Burnt Ash Lane opposite Sundridge Parade. One of its funder members, Nobby Buckingham, recalled its being built in 1927. Over the years it grew and in 1978 a major extension was added. The club is affiliated to the CIU. The Chairman in 2012 is Albert Crowhurst; membership is around 800 which now includes female members. At the AGM in 2010 it was resolved that women could join in their own right. The club has a lively programme of social events and large function rooms for members' celebrations.

Fig. 35 Tennis courts at King's Meadow in 1932 with St Andrew's Hall, then brand new, visible to the left. *Photo: From archives of the late John Malcolm Smith*

As to the origin of the name 'King's Meadow' we can do no better that note that Horsburgh records that the King family owned a house of the site of Hall's Farm in the 16th Century, so there is a possibility that what is now King's Meadow Recreation Ground may well have been his meadow, as at that time there would have been no railway embankment obstructing his path.

7

The Building of St Andrew's

In the 1920's St Mary's Church regularly had collections until the permanent Church of St Andrew's was built. In 1926 an appeal was launched for funds to support the venture and on 7th February 1927 the ecclesiastical parish of St Andrew's Bromley was granted by Order in Council with the Rev. J M T Griffiths becoming the first vicar of the parish.

The first combined Vestry and Parochial Church meeting took place on 26th April, 1927. Messrs F H Sherriff and C Sheldon were elected churchwardens and those elected to the first Parochial Church Council were Mr S J Andrews, Mrs Asbury, Miss Chambers, Mr J Huckle, Mr C Hughesman, Mr J Lamb, Mr B G Parkerson, Mrs Reeve, Miss Sheldon, Mrs Sherriff, Mr H M Singleton, Mr F J Stanger, Mrs Tolhurst, Miss G Willis and Mr F Wise. Mrs Chater and Mrs Lawdon-Eaton were elected as representatives to the Ruridecanal Conference.

Fig. 36 Site of St Andrew's church in 1929 before a brick was laid; the 'Tin Church' in the background on the opposite side of Burnt Ash Lane   *Photo: St Andrew's archives*

In March 1928 the site of the new church was finally confirmed. After a false start looking at an alternative site in Burnt Ash Lane, in March it was finally resolved to purchase the vacant plot next to the Working Men's Club as the site of the new church from Mr Albert Frampton at a cost of £1,250. Again Bessie Bartholomew takes up the story'

'Then began a period of great activity, with the forming of a St Andrew's Building Committee, and the arranging by our own people of sales, garden fêtes, miles of pennies, and so on, to raise money for the new church. The most generous example set by St Mary's in putting aside a first £2,000 towards the new building and the housing of its minister was followed by the whole Church community of Bromley, and the holding in the grounds of Bromley College of a two-day fête, organized by the Churches of the Bromley Deanery in aid of our building fund, and opened by the Marchioness of Camden, accompanied by the Marquis of Camden, Lord Lieutenant of the County, was evidence of the spirit of co-operation and enthusiasm which prevailed. Another stimulus was that St Andrew's was the first of the new churches in the diocese to be associated with the Twelve Churches Fund, the object of which was to supplement local effort to meet the spiritual needs of the growing population of areas undergoing development.

'In 1929 work on the new church began, and on 27th July of that year, in the presence of the Bishop of Rochester (Dr J R Harmer) who conducted the religious service, the architect (Sir Charles Nicholson), over three hundred Freemasons in full regalia, and a large gathering of clergy and church people, the foundation stone was laid.

Fig. 37   The foundation stone laying ceremony 1929   *Photo: St Andrew's archives*

The stone is in the west wall, on the left-hand side of the door, and is inscribed, "A M D G (To the greater glory of God). This foundation stone was laid with Masonic ceremony by the Provincial Grand Master for Kent, Lord Cornwallis, CBE, and blessed by the Bishop of the Diocese, July 27, 1929". On the lower part of the stone is engraved the Masonic symbol, the square and compasses. A cavity in the stone contains coins of the realm, copies of the *Church Times* and *St* Andrews's *Magazine* and the day's Order of Service.

Fig. 38 Rt Rev. J R Harmer, Bishop of Rochester at the time of the building of St Andrew's Church
Photo: St Andrew's archives

'Thereafter the building of the church went steadily on, and, in anticipation of many jobs being available in and around it when it was finished, the Guild of Service was formed in January, 1930. So we come to the day when the labours and sacrifices of many people, quite a number of whom are happily still with us, were rewarded.

'Saturday 10th May, 1930, saw the consecration of the new Church of St Andrew, Burnt Ash Lane, Bromley, a building which, in my experience, never fails to evoke admiration from visitors, clerical or lay. The consecration service, with its impressive ceremonial, was conducted by the Bishop of Rochester, attended by more than thirty clergy and the choirs of St Mary's and St Andrew's, in the presence of a congregation so large that many could not find even standing room within and remained outside the open doors.

'Many of the furnishings and ornaments were gifts; the pulpit came from St Mary's, the brass cross and candlesticks on the high altar given by St Mark's, the font was bought with farthings giving by children of St Andrew's, and the sanctuary lamp was the gift of the Guild of Service. The lectern, which the Rev. G E Parsons gave us in his time, is a fine piece of work, being carved out of a single block of oak.

'The war shrine on the wall above the font originally stood on the roadway. It was moved to the new church from the 'tin church'

'The church was free of debt within about one year of its opening, and of the sum of £11,000 which it cost including the land, about £6,000 was raised locally in Bromley and neighbourhood.

'The old iron church which had served us so well was used for a while as a church hall, but plans for the erection of a new hall adjacent to the church were soon formed and put in hand, and in December, 1931, the present church hall was opened by the Bishop of Rochester. The stage and some of the floor boards from the old hall were used in the building of the new one.'

Fig. 39 St Andrew's Church in 1932 with the church hall in the background
Photo: St Andrew's archives

The necessity for additional clerical assistance was soon realised, and an assistant clergy fund was started, with the result that the Rev. R W Walls came as the first curate at Harvest, 1935, remaining for three years, when he was succeeded by the Rev. N D Walker.

The whole-hearted support from St Mary's for the fledgling parish of St Andrew's is hard to over-state. Rev. Gowans, the long-serving vicar of St Mary's was a man of considerable musical talents; he had a fine bass voice, could play the organ, and while Rector of Smeaton, near Whitby, he conducted the combined choirs taking part in the music festivals at Whitby. When he came to St Mary's, Plaistow, he took a keen interest in maintaining an already high standard of musicianship at his new parish.

Fig. 40 (Left to right)
1 Frank Stanger (standing), 2 Mr Sheldon (sitting), 3 Fred Wise, 4 (?), 5 Mrs Lewis,
6 Rev. J M T Griffiths, 7 Mrs Stanger snr, 8 Mrs Mylton, 9 Mrs Willey, 10 Mrs Lamb,
11 Mrs Chater, 12 (?), 13 Mr Mylton

Photo: St Andrew's archives

This enthusiasm must have transmitted itself to St Andrew's, judging by the huge choir shown in Fig. 21.

Rev. Gowans died on 3rd April 1941 and at the memorial service Canon Hassard-Short remarked that the great event of his long incumbency at St Mary's was the creation of the parish of St Andrew's.

The close association of the Freemasonry movement with the early days of St Andrew's is of more than passing interest.

At the time of the building of the church, it was the then Lord Bishop of Rochester, the Rev. Dr J R Harmer, past Grand Chaplain of England, who conducted the foundation stone-laying ceremony. He was an Hon. member of the Manor of Bromley Lodge it was at his suggestion that an invitation was issued to the Lord Cornwallis CBE to take a prominent role in the ceremonies, with the full concurrence of the incumbent. Lord Cornwallis was the Provincial Grand Master for Kent and Deputy Grand Master of England.

The names of the dignitaries who attended were recorded for posterity by the *Kentish Times* of 2nd August 1929.

8
1939 - 1945

In 1940 the Rev. J M T Griffiths accepted the living of Rusthall, and the Rev. S H Cooke was inducted Vicar of St Andrew's on 25th July, 1940. In the following year the Rev. M W Dittmer took Mr Walker's place as curate, remaining until Easter, 1943. Fr Cooke had previously been a schoolmaster at Bromsgrove, and after training for the priesthood at Mirfield became curate at Northfleet from 1935-1940.

Charles Clarke, writing for the 'Burning Bush' in April 1980 recalled events from the war years onwards.

Fig. 41 Rev. S H Cooke
Photo: St Andrew's archives

'Although the war affected everyone in various ways the services at St Andrew's continued with the minimum of change. The windows of the choir vestry were bricked up so that it could be used as an air raid shelter and, during the winter months, the early morning services were held there. The black-out requirements also made it necessary to have evening services at 3.15 during the winter months and the Christmas midnight communion was ruled out until 1942 when a special relaxation allowed us to have it with only two candles on the altar and a red light bulb at the back of the church.

'Only minor damage was suffered by the church during the war and services were suspended for only a few days while an unexploded parachute bomb in the cemetery was attended to. One of the few references to the war in the PCC minutes mentions that three mattresses and six blankets were purchased for the comfort of the ladies engaged on fire-watching in the church.

'Early in 1942 Mr Cooke left on war service and Mr Walls was invited back as priest-in-charge. He remained until the end of 1944 when the Rev. K T Makin took over until the vicar's return in May 1946. On Armistice Sunday 1946 there was a special service attended by the Scouts and Guides and members of the Home Guard when the Book of Remembrance was dedicated; this book includes

Fig. 42 Rev. R W Walls
Photo: Win Snell archive

the names not only of members of the forces and the fire service but also civilians who were killed in or near their homes in the parish and a member of the Home Guard killed on duty in Bromley.' The book is inscribed:-

'There is music in the midst of desolation
And a glory that shines upon our tears'

Those commemorated are listed below. In the Book of Remembrance they are listed randomly; below they are listed from the beginning to the end of World War II, then those who fell in later conflicts. The Blitz attack on the night of 16th/17th April 1941 saw the destruction of the block of flats and houses in Southover, in which sixteen people lost their lives, and must count as the blackest night in the entire history of the Burnt Ash area. Those in italics do not appear in the Book of Remembrance but are listed in 'Civilian War Dead' published by the Imperial War Graves Commission in 1954.

1940

Pte Albert Dell, aged 22, of the RWK Regt., killed in action in France on 16th June 1940

Pte John Bertram Ecott, aged 25, of the RASC, who served in the NAAFI, was a victim of the sinking of the Troopship HMT Lancastria off the coast of France during the evacuation in June 1940. The Ecott family lived in Hilldrop Road.

May Louise Greatwood, aged 61, of 34, Alexandra Crescent, daughter of Mr & Mrs W. Anwell of Clapham, London; wife of Herbert H Greatwood, killed during an air raid on 7th Sep. 1940, a member of the Mothers' Union

George Elliott Gilpin, aged 59, Air Raid Warden, husband of Bessie G.W. Gilpin, of 68 Alexandra Crescent, killed on duty at 14, Alexandra Crescent on 7th Sep. 1940

Thomas Alfred Mulley, aged 51, and *Elizabeth Ann Mulley*, aged 52, of 7, Hillcrest Road. Thomas died on 7th October 1940, at 7, Hillcrest Road, and Elizabeth of injuries, later the same day, at Bromley and District Hospital

Ernest Riches Titus Champion, aged 40, of 20, Hilldrop Rd, son of Thomas Henry and Emily Elizabeth Champion, of 110, Burnt Ash Lane, on 7th October 1940, at Holmesdale Rd

Jane Eliza Wells, aged 50? Of 7, Hillcrest Rd, on 11th October 1940, at 7, Hillcrest Rd

Harold George Jerome, aged 32, of the National Fire Service, husband of E.M. Jerome, of 86, Burnt Ash Lane, killed on duty during an air raid on 2nd Nov. 1940 at Springfield Fire Station.

John James Taylor, aged 27, Fireman, AFS, 32, Portland Road, son of Ebenezer John and Irene Mary Taylor of 13, Glebe Rd, husband of Winifred Clara Taylor, died on 2nd November 1940, at Springhill Fire Station., College Rd.

1941

Raymond Eric Willey, aged 34, a volunteer in the Home Guard, killed on duty during an air raid on 16th Apr. 1941, a sidesman and server. He was killed on his way to report for duty at the police station as was Volunteer **R T Sharp**.

Louisa Matilda Sutch, aged 48, widow of Edward Bert Sutch, of 52 Southover, and her children **Ivy Louisa**, aged 18, **James Frederick,** aged 16, **Dorothy Ethel,** aged 14, **and Edna Vera,** aged 11, killed at Southover during an air raid on 16th Apr. 1941

Dorothy Ethel Hopgood, aged 12, of 64, Southover, a member of the Sunday School, and her parents **Reginald,** aged 45 **and Caroline Elizabeth**, aged 46, killed at 64, Southover in an air raid on 16th Apr. 1941

Daniel Russell, aged 17, of 58, Southover, son of Mr W. Russell, on 16th April 1941, at 58, Southover

Reginald Thomas Sharp, aged 16, Home Guard, son of Samuel B and Sarah R Sharp, of 15, Lushington Road, Catford, on 16th April 1941 at Southover

Ethel Florence Childs, aged 28, of 62, Southover, daughter of George and Rose Fairy, of 25, Rosevere Rd, Grove Park, wife of Arthur Charles Childs, HM Forces, and their sons *Arthur Derek,* aged 4 and *Tony William*, aged 2 on 16th April 1941 at 62, Southover (According to *Bromley in the Front Line* by Lewis Blake).

Ellen Elizabeth Steel, aged 43, and her daughter *Patricia Rose*, aged 5, of 54, Southover, on 16th April 1941, at Southover

1942

Pte Charles James Williams aged 26, of the RAMC, presumed killed in a military hospital in Singapore, Feb. 1942

Sgt Wm. James Davies, aged 34, of the RAF, killed in action over Belgium on 17th Sep. 1942

1943

Sgt Lionel Robert Wallace, aged 20, of the RAF, presumed killed in action over the English Channel on 7th Apr. 1943, a former choirboy

Gnr Cecil Frederick Hillier, aged 21, of the RA, the Maritime Marine Service, killed in action at sea on 10th Apr. 1943, a former member of the Bible Class

L.Bdr Henry James Frederick Horley, aged 28, of the R A, died in a POW camp in Thailand on 7th Aug. 1943, a former choirboy

LAC Herbert Davies, aged 25, of the RAF died on active service in India on 21st Sep. 1943

William Chadwick, aged 38, husband of Nellie Chadwick, of 20, Brook Lane, on 7th October 1943, at Bromley South Station

Gnr Reginald Kewell, aged 27, of the RA, died in a POW hospital in Thailand in Dec. 1943

1944

Lieut Antony Gwyndam Gwyn Gaisford, aged 21, of the Black Watch, killed in action at Bruk, Holland, on 8th Feb. 1944

Flt Sgt John Gorringe Pollard, aged 21, of the RAF, presumed killed in action over the Dutch coast, 21st Feb. 1944

Pte Harold Norman Judd, aged 30, of the 2nd Bn Border Regiment, killed in action in Burma on 18th March 1944, a former choirboy and member of the Men's Club

Sgt Percival George Binder, aged 21, of the RAF, presumed killed in action over Nuremburg on 31st Mar. 1944

Pte Leonard John Bloss, aged 25, of the Lincolnshire Regt, killed in action in Burma on 7th Apr. 1944, a member of the choir and the Guild of Service

Rfn Gordon Henry Markham, aged 26, of the Rifle Brigade, killed in action on 16th Apr. 1944

SLt (A) Stanley Frederick Such, aged 23, of the RNVR, killed in action over L'Aberwrach, France, on 1st May 1944 (see below)

Pte Ronald Frederick Groombridge, aged 19, of the Queen's Royal Rgt, killed in action in Burma on 13th May 1944

FO Francis Robert Marsh, of the RAF, missing on active service on 29th May 1944. FO Marsh died aged 22; he was the son of Francis and Eliza Anna Marsh, of Bromley. He has no known grave but is remembered with honour on the Runnymede Memorial, Surrey, Panel 287. In 2012 Janet Mayberry (née Marsh) presented St Andrew's with a new nave altar in memory of her late father and mother Francis and Betty Marsh.

Lieut David Brooke, aged 20, of the East Riding Yeomanry, killed in action in Normandy on 9th June 1944

Alfred Hebberton Sheldon, aged 47, his wife **Marjorie** and their daughter **Hilary**, of 34, Treewall Gardens, on 27th June 1944 at 34, Treewall Gardens

Catherine Mary Burke, aged 3, of 32 Treewall Gardens, daughter of Richard Anthony Bernard and Emily Burke, at 32, Treewall Gardens on 27th June 1944

Pte Douglas Arthur Day, aged 18, of the Devonshire Regt, died of wounds while on active service in France on 2nd Aug. 1944, a former member of the Bible Class

FO Sidney Charles Hubbard DFM, aged 30, of the RAF killed in action on 6th Aug. 1944

Christopher Benjamin Oastler, aged 46, of 243, Keedonwood Road, on 8th August 1944, at Bromley & District Hospital.

Gnr Edwin Kewell, aged 25, of the RA, died, a POW in Japanese hands on 12th Sep. 1944, a member of the Guild of Service

Lieut Donald William Bulley, aged 23, of the 2nd Fife and Forfar Yeomanry, killed in action in North West Europe on 22nd Sep. 1944

FO Henry George Arbon, aged 22 years, of the RAF, presumed killed in action over Germany on 4th Nov. 1944, a sidesman, member of the Guild of Service and of the Mens' Club

1945

Driver Harry Thomas Bushby, aged 37, of the RASC, died of injuries while on active service in Belgium on 4th Jan 1945, a former choirboy

FO Arthur William Higginson, aged 21, of the RAF, killed in action over Germany on 22nd Feb. 1945, a member of the choir

AB James Sussex, aged 24, of the RN, presumed killed in action while on convoy duty on 26th Mar. 1945

L/Cpl Frank Howard Wordley, aged 29, of the RASC, died in a POW camp in Japan on 10th Mar. 1945

L/Cpl Albert Edward Howe, aged 29, of 187 Field Amb. RASC, died on 13th April 1945 and is buried at Jonkerbos War Cemetery, Netherlands Grave Ref. 21.C.2 He was the husband of Gladys Dora Howe of Peckham.

William Leslie Newton, aged 18 years, died on National Service in the mines on 16th Oct. 1945

SLt (A) Peter Benjamin Garrett, aged 20, of the RNVR, died from injuries received in a flying accident on 24th Nov. 1945

1953

2Lt David William Manning, 1st Btn. The Queen's Own Royal West Kent Regt., died of wounds received in action in Malaya, St George's Day, 23rd Apr. 1953, a member of the Guild of Service

One of the earliest fatalities, that of Pte John Bertram Ecott, on 17th June 1940 links St Andrew's with sinking of the troopship HMT Lancastria off St Nazaire, the French Atlantic port at the mouth of the Loire. The sinking was the most catastrophic maritime disaster of the entire war, and loss of life exceeded that in the sinking of the Lusitania and the Titanic combined. Such was the scale of the disaster that Churchill, through the D Notice system, blocked all reporting in the press and on radio. The number who perished will never be known but Bert Ecott was just one of approximately 6,000 who lost their lives. By coincidence Mr Ron Becconsall's cousin, WO2 Frederick J Puddicombe, of RASC, who also served in NAAFI, and who lived at Cross Road, Bromley Common went down with the same ship.

On the first night of the Blitz, 7th September 1940, George Elliott Gilpin an Air Raid Warden was killed while on duty and May Louise Greatwood was also killed.

By the time the Blitz had run its course 79 days later Harold George Jerome had also been killed whilst on duty with the National Fire Service.

Over and above those whose names appear in the St Andrew's Remembrance Book, there are at least 13 casualties of World War II who are commemorated on grave-stones/memorials in Plaistow Cemetery, Bromley. These are:

1941

Sgt Edwin Jones Bonney, aged 27, RAF, who died on 22nd January 1941.

Leading Seaman Roy D Waters, aged 22, Royal Navy, lost at sea 9th April 1941, serving on HMS Voltaire. He was the son of David and Eleanor Waters, of Farnborough, Kent. David had lost his life in the Great War, so this family lost father and son in the two wars.

Sgt David Hinton Howe, aged 24, RAFVR, died on 6th August 1941

1942

Pte Leslie John Rowe, aged 18, QORWK Regt, died on 27th May 1942

1943

Aircraftman 2nd Cl. Leonard Victor Young, ages 21, RAFVR died on 10th September 1943.

L/Bmbr Henry William Rowley, aged 52, Royal Artillery who died on 12th September 1943.

1944

Pte Douglas Arthur Day, aged 18, Dorsetshire Regt, died on 2nd August 1944

1945

Pte George Frederick Humphries, Pioneer Corps, died on 14th January 1945

Sgt (Flt Eng.) Peter Henry Morris, RAF Volunteer Reserve who died on 28th January 1945

Bmbr George Olof Larsen, aged 26, Royal Artillery, died on 13th March 1945 On the grave-stone his regimental affiliation is given as '34th Bn QORWK and Searchlight Regt RA'

LAC Ronald Taylor, aged 23, RAFVR, died on 25th April 1945

Sub. Lieut Peter Benjamin Garrett, aged 20, RNVR died on 24th November 1945

1947

Trooper Leonard Charles Lane, aged 35, Royal Armoured Corps who died on 8th January 1947 (Grave M 120)

Pte Sidney Albert Osborn, aged 39, Army Catering Corps, died on 10th October 1947

Rangefield Mission, Rangefield Road (now closed) commemorated four of their number who fell during WW2. These were:

Spr William Henry Cole, aged 25, 215 Field Coy RE, died 22nd February 1943. His parents were Thomas Henry and Ellen Louisa Cole and he was husband to Maria Louise Cole, of Bromley.

AB Alfred John Cronin, age unknown, who died on 23rd February 1942, serving with the RN on HM Submarine Tempest. His parents were Frederick John and Emma Elizabeth Cronin of Catford, London and he was the husband of Florence Mavis Cronin also of Catford.

Sgt Charles Raymond Francis, age unknown, with 357 Sqdn RAFVR, who died on 30th July 1945, commemorated in Singapore. He was the son of Leonard Jack and Evelyn May Francis of Catford, London

L/Sgt Edward George Stuppel, aged 25, 4th Field Regiment, RA who died on 17th January 1944. His parents were Edward John and Ellen Ruth Stuppel of Pimlico, London.

I am indebted to Patricia Knowlden for the following paragraphs. Her highly informative little book *The Long Alert 1937-1945* published in 1988 provided an insight into the impact of the war on the Burnt Ash area of Bromley. Her father Mr Reginald Gedye was the local district Civil Defence warden, having enrolled in the Air Raid Precaution scheme in 1938. He was in charge of Group 2, the northern half of Plaistow Electoral Ward and the tip of Sundridge, lying on either side of Burnt Ash Lane. By the end of July 1939 Bromley had been divided into 17 groups or areas with Head Wardens, each with 5-10 sectors. The first meeting of Group 2 (later 1A) was held on 30th October 1938 at the Burnt Ash Lane Working Men's Club and was attended by six wardens including Mr Gedye who chaired the meeting. Training was always a major topic for discussion, which covered numerous areas such as the warning system, messages, protection from bombs, maps and local knowledge, relations with police, public and other services and first aid. The group adopted the motto 'Nulli secundus' and 'RG' and his team worked tirelessly to justify it.

At the beginning of 1939 recruitment to civil defence was at full tilt, building up to a total of 1,000, comprising 700 wardens, 22 first aid parties, 7 rescue parties and 7 gas decontamination squads. At a meeting at St Andrew's Church Hall the wardens dressed up in their yellow gas-proof oilskins with gum-boots and respirators, and thirty or forty of the audience were so impressed that they signed up there and then.

District 1A had 4 brick posts fitted with telephones and were manned as action stations on the yellow alert. One was in the playground of Burnt Ash School, the others were at the Westminster School playing fields (Thornton Road), New Street Hill opposite the junction with Oak Tree Gardens and Lewisham boundary.

After an uneventful spring in 1941, Bromley found itself right in the front line: on the evening of Wednesday 16th April a lone raider dropped a chandelier flare over the town, the preliminary to a full-scale air attack. Patricia remembered, cooped up in their shelter, the throbbing drone of aero engines round and round over their heads instead of passing over. The rapid pom-pom of the anti-aircraft gun that ran up and down the railway line was much more frequent than usual, and a peep outside showed the searchlight beams waving about like some kind of demented aurora borealis.

'The flare had been followed by the drop of thousands of incendiaries and soon the H Es (high explosive bombs) followed Some sounded very close to us although, as usual, they did not all go off. Then, just before midnight, there was a terrific bang and everything shook – including us! – but we had no way of knowing what had happened, or how far away. Of course we worried about my father, out in it all; it did not seem possible that any human body could have moved unscathed through what was gone on out there. On his rounds, he dropped in once to see how we were, but said little. He looked tired and drawn. Gradually, through the small hours of Thursday, the attack lessened, and periods of quiet grew longer, and at last those undaunted cocks greeted the grey daylight spreading abroad to reveal the damage that had been done; the all-clear sounded, and we emerged stiffly from our hole to breathe in lung-fulls of new sweet air. Never was dawn so welcome.

Of the 55 bombs that fell on District 1A altogether, 18 fell during that raid, but although much damage was done to property and the railway line severed, they only caused one serious incident: one man was trapped under the ruins of his house, but he was dug out and taken to hospital with crushed ribs and a perforated ear-drum, and made a good recovery.

The big explosion we heard at midnight was a different matter. A parachute mine had demolished a block of flats in Southover, trapping people inside the building, some alive and some dead. The post warden recounted his experience:

"The mine exploded at 2400 hrs. The first casualty I saw was a woman with a gashed head, who rushed up to me covered in blood, clutching my coat and imploring me to do something for her. I attended to her injuries first and then got to the site, rescuing and attending to casualties etc. Twenty minutes elapsed before the report went off (to control). Communications had broken down, so a messenger was sent off with an express report to Springhill Stretcher Party Depot, for them to phone Bromley Control. I then sent a verbal report by messenger on a bike to Control, telling them we wanted rescue and stretcher parties. I was told there were people buried underneath the debris and heard a woman's voice say 'Warden! I can see your light'. A man standing by said 'I'll move around, tell me if you can still see the light'. He did so and there was a shout from the woman that he was standing on her chest. There were 19 people buried under the debris and three or four were got out and the minor casualties to Keedonwood Road trenches before the rescue party arrived and everyone else left unless asked by them to stay. A small fire started under some of the debris, sufficient to be dangerous, so fire parties worked on it with stirrup pumps, and a chain of buckets was passed to keep up the water supply.

72

Fig. 43 Anderson shelter in garden of 216 Keedonwood Road   *drawn by George Church*

It was necessary, however, to send for the fire brigade. They were some time coming and someone suggested using a hose, but this was dangerous. If you put down a quantity of water onto burning debris, you may drown those buried beneath. The fire brigade could not play the hose for the same reason.

We found three people dead and wedged in the debris and could not be moved; we had to send for a doctor to remove them and get to those behind who were still alive. One was a Mrs Leaper, who was pregnant six months. She was quite all right and has since had her baby and is very thankful to the Warden's Service for what they did.

The assistant engineer arrived and had a look at No. 66; we did not go to No. 64 because the person next door said that the Hopgoods were quite all right and had gone to Bromley.

The rescuing went on until 12 o'clock the next day, the wardens working in relays with two or three hours off then returning. I returned to the site to clear off some looters and pilferers and saw Mrs Hopgood's sister, who said that something must have happened to the family as they were not in Bromley and would have been to see her if they were all right. It was decided to search the debris at the back of the house and, the wardens having left, a home guard helped. At first there was no sign but after working a way in at the back downstairs, a hand could be seen sticking out through the kitchen. We shifted the debris and could see the mother and daughter. I sent for the rescue party again. They came back and cleared out three people. The whole family was wiped out."

On that night George Church was in the Anderson shelter at the bottom of his garden in Keedonwood Road with his father and mother and brother Alan, when they heard the huge blast nearby in Southover. They emerged at the all clear to find that their front door was completely blown off its hinges. As an indication of the peculiarity of bomb blast, his windows were intact and only his door was blown in but not those of his neighbours. A characteristic of the blast from land mines was that when the detonation probes struck the ground and the mine exploded, the blast force was horizontal which is why they created such widespread devastation. There was no crater. Like so many in the area, the Church's house was also hit by incendiaries which set fire to the roof, but was dealt with by the fire brigade. In all nine flats and three houses were destroyed and nearly 500 damaged.

On the same night another parachute mine fell in Plaistow Cemetery but became entangled in a tree and failed to detonate. Doris Burford, living in Gladwell Road and her neighbours from the area around the cemetery were evacuated at 2 a.m. and made their way to a Church in Widmore Road where they were given temporary accommodation. She remembers going there with Bill Morris, who was always singing, even in the darkest days of the war. Bearing in mind the devastation caused that night in Southover and Nichol Lane, that tree was all that stood in the way of similar carnage in Gladwell, Hilldrop and Foxbury Roads and Burnt Ash Lane all of which bordered on the cemetery.

This account was given at a "special meeting to discuss the experiences of the 'Big Raid' in order to learn from them."

Seventy-four people died in Bromley on the night of 16th April, which was also the night that the Parish Church of SS Peter & Paul was hit by a mine and destroyed except for the tower. Patricia noted that one of her school-friends was killed there.

Lewis Blake, author of *Bromley in the Front Line* recorded that this was 18-year-old Hazel Kissick of Bromley County Girls' School, a grim reminder that 16-18-year-olds were required to serve in something positive for the war effort, despite the risks. Of the 74 who were killed that night, 48 were victims of the bombing of Nichol Lane, Southover, Lansdowne Road and Babbacombe Road.

As the CD Controller later wrote to his personnel, "The night of 16th-17th April (1941) brought a test of a magnitude not exceeded in any town in the country, having regard to our size and population and the way it was overcome is a credit to all concerned. Due to your leadership, organising ability and training methods…. and devotion to duty. Well done, we can take it and we will still go to it."

On that fateful night the Hopgood and Sutch families were wiped out and Raymond John Willey was also killed.

Nine flats and three houses were destroyed and nearly 500 damaged.

Just after midnight another HE fell with disastrous results in Nichol Lane. 19 people were killed in the Nichol Lane blast, the mine falling to the rear of No. 72, the home of the Randalls, a well-known golfing family. Percy Randall, aged 43, his brother William, aged 49, and their sister, Helen aged 65 were among the fatalities.

Fig. 44 Site of the bombing of Nichol Lane, viewed from the Hadlow's Garage.
The Prince Frederick extreme left of photo. *Courtesy: Bromley Central Library*

The Mummery family lost five members: husband, wife, two infant sons and Mr Mummery's sister. With the destruction of 26 houses and severe damage to seventy more, devastation scarred Nichol Lane and Croft Road for many years afterwards. Another resident of Nichol Lane who lost his life was Stanley Thomas Frank Burton, 31, fire-watcher, son of T C and A A Burton of 14, North Street, Bromley, husband of Julian Mary Burton, who lived at No. 78 but happened to be visiting his father when a bomb dropped to the rear of 14, North Street on 31st January 1941.

The parish boundary between St Andrew's and St Mary's runs down the centre of Nichol Lane. By a quirk of fate, it appears that all the fatalities were suffered the row of houses between Nos. 66 and 75, all of which were on the St Mary's side of the street plus other fatalities in Lychet Road, which backs on to Nichol Lane.

The names of all nineteen people who perished on that dreadful night are listed below

Joanna Ahearne, aged 28, of Sundridge Ave., on 16th April 1941, at 1 Lychet Rd

Sarah Ann Burrows, aged 69, of 74, Nichol Lane, on 16th April 1941, at 74, Nichol Lane

Lawrence Walter Byerley, aged 26, of 75, Nichol Lane, on 16th April 1941 at 75, Nichol Lane

Gordon Harold Frank Cox, aged 19, of 66, Nichol Lane, son of Mr & Mrs Sydney George Cox, on 16th April 1941 at 66, Nichol Lane

June Evelyn Dunn, aged 4, of 71, Nichol Lane, daughter of Charles Leslie Dunn, on 16th April 1941 at 71, Nichol Lane

William Foley, aged 35, of 1, Lychet Rd, on 16th April 1941, at Nichol Lane

John Mason, aged 30, of 1, Lychet Rd, on 16th April 1941, at Nichol Lane

Sidney Bradfield Monger, aged 56, of 74, Nichol Lane, son of the late Emma Monger of 5, Crown Lane, on 16th April 1941, at 74, Nichol Lane

Leslie Charles Mummery, aged 39, his wife *Helen*, aged 39 of 75, Nichol Lane, on 16th April 1941 at Nichol Lane

Freda May Mummery, aged 31, of 73 Nichol Lane, *Ronald Ernest*, aged 4, and *Brian Leslie*, aged 12 months, sons of A.E. and Freda Mummery, on 16th April 1941 at 73, Nichol Lane

Mrs Lily Ettie Pettifor, aged 31, of 1, Lychet Rd, on 16th April 1941, at 1, Lychet Rd

Helen Louise Randall, aged 65, and her brothers *Percy Cyril Randall*, aged 43 and *William James Randall*, aged 49, of 72, Nichol Lane, on 16th April 1941, at 72, Nichol Lane

Evelyn May Scudder, aged 26, wife of Pte G.W. Scudder, The Leicestershire Regt., of 71, Nichol Lane, and their daughter *Gillian Ann*, on 16th April 1941, at 71, Nichol Lane

On the same night there were nine fatalities in Lansdowne Road, and six at Babbacombe Road. Three of those killed at 64, Lansdowne Rd were CID officers investigating a robbery which had taken place in Lewisham. DIs Haynes and O'Sullivan and Sgt Davey called at the house before the raid began and were still there when a large calibre bomb demolished the house killing them and several occupants.

Muriel Hinkley who lived at 43, Kynaston Road (aged 88 in 2012) remembers how, at the top of Kynaston Road, a group of neighbours organised a voluntary fire-watching patrol. 'Some contributions of money bought hose-pipes and a stirrup pump and my father organised instruction and practices on Sunday mornings outside No. 43. Incendiary bombs were greatly feared and a rota was made out so that each household was responsible for one night vigil per week. Our household comprised my father, mother, elder sister, and elder brother working as a team of four from 10 p.m. to 6 a.m., 2 hours each.

'I can well remember my mother, a gentle creature, easily flurried, was given one end of a hose-pipe to hold. She kept turning round to hear more clearly the instruction from whoever was at the stirrup pump and on each turn she thoroughly doused the people standing there! When the bomb in Southover blew out the windows of our house, I was at home. We were in the brick shelter at the bottom of the garden. Elder brother John had refused to join us but I remember his sudden flight down the garden path!

'My life-long friend, Pauline Hosking, and I were a lively, energetic pair. We explored many activities after leaving school. We were founder members of the first Girls' Naval Training Corps. We responded to the 'Dig for Victory' campaign. The Westminster School playing field at the end of Thornton Road had been turned into "10 rood" allotments. We applied to Bromley Town Hall for a half plot (5 roods). I think we had to pay 5 shillings.

Fig. 45a Civil Defence section 1940-43 mustered at the pavilion at Westminster School Playing Fields Thornton Road

Front row seated (L-R)

P W Pritchett, P W Richardson, D D W Layton, D W Gedye, P W Arnold, P W Hewett

Back row 4th from right: Hector Smith, father of Ken Smith

Photo: Courtesy Ken Smith

'I remember giggly Pauline arriving at No. 43 with a large spade. I collected one from our garden shed and we marched to Thornton Road to find our plot. We were completely ignorant with no gardening knowledge or experience at all! The allotment scheme was well under way and some men had already prepared ground for planting. Pauline and I stood by our marked-out numbered plot and wondered *how* to tackle the great expanse of grass that was now our responsibility.

'We were helpless young girls. A man on the next plot took pity on us. He came across and expertly removed with his sharp spade a rectangle of turf, put it aside, dug out earth, buried the turf (double digging). It looked so easy. Gradually our plot became fit for planting but I cannot remember how much hard work was done for us by kind gardening neighbours and how much was our own effort.'

'Pauline and I joined the WRVS and the first produce from our plot was harvested by my mother.'

Muriel married Sub-Lieutenant Stanley Frederick Such of the RNVR on February 13th 1944 at St Andrew's Church (Fig. 47). Stanley who was a Fleet Air Arm pilot, went missing believed killed over L'Aberwrach, near Brest on North French coast on 1st May. It was several weeks before she received confirmation that he had indeed perished. He had tragically come down with two other allied aircraft on the waterfront. He was aged only 23. They had been married for less than three months.

Muriel herself had trained as a radar mechanic and was occupied on what was then hush-hush work removing, repairing and testing aircraft radar equipment.

With the advent of the V1 Flying Bomb (commonly referred to as the doodlebug or buzz-bomb) in 1944 came the threat of indiscriminate bombing of civilian targets. Lewis Blake in *Bromley in the Front Line* says that on 15th-16th June 1944 the bombardment began in earnest at about 11.30 p.m. and 24 hours later 250 buzz-bombs had been launched. 180 crossed the south coast and some 70 fell in the London region, including 10 or so shot down by AA gunfire. South East London received the brunt of the attack; a pattern that would be repeated through that indifferent summer.

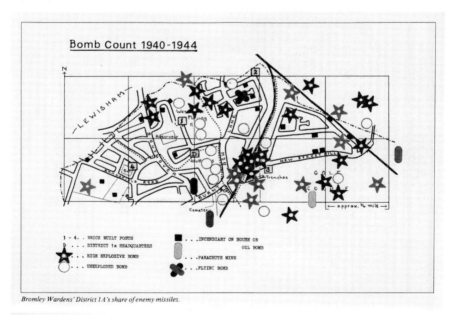

Bromley Wardens' District 1A's share of enemy missiles.

Fig. 45b Bomb Count 1940-1944 Civil Defence area 1A from 'The Long Alert 1937-1945 by Patricia Knowlden

'During one eleven-week period some 250 V1s fell in the Bromley area and perhaps another 1000 passed overhead.

'Many local residents went back to the old Blitz routine of spending nights in shelters.

'The old Borough of Bromley was the target for 37 flying bombs.

These included the bomb which destroyed 32-36 Treewall Gardens on 27th June 1944. Fire broke out in the debris and 440 houses in the area were damaged. Three people were killed at No. 32. The Remembrance Book at St Andrew's identifies them as Alfred Hebberton Sheldon, his wife Marjorie and their daughter Hilary.

Kath and Malcolm Goodwin identified the houses in Fig. 41. The semi-detached house to the extreme right of the photo is the rear of No. 64 Ridgeway Drive, (the air-raid shelter in the back garden was later demolished); the next house is the rear of their house, No. 62. Next is the end-terrace No. 60, two mid-terrace and the other end terrace.

Patricia Knowlden mentions that next door to the Sheldons was the Burke family of mother, father daughter and son. The Burkes lost their daughter, but the entire Sheldon family was wiped out.

'The last flying bombs fell on Bromley on 14th August 1944 but were replaced in November by the V2 rockets which struck with no warning at all; the nearest to the St Andrew's parish struck Lewisham.

Fig. 46 Bomb damage in Treewall Gardens
Courtesy: Bromley Central Library

The V2 attacks became more sporadic as our armies, now on the continent, pushed the enemy back from the coast and the launching pads, and the last rocket fell on Bromley on 26th March 1945.

Patricia Knowlden quotes from a letter from Mr George Sheldon, brother of Alfred Sheldon, who was killed by the flying bomb. Writing to her father, he said "The wardens were performing a difficult, dangerous, and most exacting job in a modest and magnificent manner, in the true tradition of civic service."

'Not only the wardens but all the branches of Civil Service "took it", and dealt with it together, until the long battle to protect their homes and families and those of their neighbours – their way of life – came at last to an end. They had more than "held on", they had filled "the unforgiving minute with sixty seconds' worth of distance run'

As soon as peace was declared the 21 year-old war widow Muriel Such made the arduous journey by rail, 3rd class, via Paris to the west Normandy coast to see her late husband's grave, returning home with the wooden cross from the site. Stanley's remains were transferred to a large military cemetery under the aegis of the War Graves Commission.

Fig. 47 Muriel Hinkley outside St Andrew's church on the day of her wedding to Stanley Such

In December 1944 her son Andrew was born. Eight years later Muriel met the man who was to become her second husband, Jack Hinkley, a senior scientist at Harwell and eventually the Atomic Power Station at Hinkley Point, near Bridgewater.

It is probably not widely known that there are other memorials to the fallen of WW2 within St Andrew's parish. Reference to Fig. 82 shows that the parish boundary cuts across Grove Park Cemetery, Marvels Lane.

Fig. 48 Military memorial, Grove Park cemetery   *Photo: Andrew Martin*

This is administered by Lewisham Borough Council but part of it lies within St Andrew's parish, including a large memorial commemorating those in Deptford who died resulting from enemy action and a World War II military memorial. On the military memorial are the names of 21 casualties buried elsewhere in the cemetery and 11 casualties commemorated on CWGC grave-stones who lie overseas. Those were from New Cross, Rotherhithe, Borough (Southwark), Deptford and Brockley. They are finally commemorated within the parish Boundary of St Andrew's, Bromley.

It is clear, beyond doubt, that the combined impact on the local communities of both World Wars was extremely severe. The whole country suffered and the communities centring on the Hollow Bottom, Burnt Ash and Sundridge Park areas were no exception.

Footnote Just prior to publication a peculiar situation came to light relating to the boundary of St Andrew's parish on the eastern side of the London-Sevenoaks railway line (see Fig. 82). Notification of a parish boundary change was published in the London Gazette of 23rd December 1938 under which a triangle of land, including part of the Grove Park Cemetery, but no dwellings, became part of St Andrew's parish. A-Z Geographia confirms that the present (2012) London/Bromley boundary was moved in 1993/4 so that the entire cemetery fell in the London area. Ecclesiastical boundaries are not necessarily coterminous with civic boundaries and it would take another Order in Council for the parish boundaries to change. This is unlikely to happen without some over-riding ecclesiastical reason for doing so. As far as is known, no change in the St Andrew's parish boundary has appeared in the London Gazette, so, on the assumption that the parish boundary shown in Fig. 82 is correct, the military memorial remains within St Andrew's parish.

Fig. 49 Southover 2012; the old elm is no more   *Photo: Andrew Martin*

9

Post War

A notable event during Rev. S H Cooke's incumbency was the publication in January 1947 of a new parish magazine called the "Burning Bush". Its cover, which was designed by a corporal of the RAF on service in Italy, included a representation of the bush that burned with fire but was nor consumed, in the vision of which Moses became aware of the presence of God and gained inspiration to deliver Israel and to lead them through the wilderness to the Promised Land. This symbol was used "to express the hope that at St Andrew's men and women may become aware of the presence of God, and walking in the light of His presence, go forth to lead others in the ways of true religion through this difficult world to the Kingdom of God". The cover, which was printed in red and green, lasted until January 1953 when printing costs required a simpler design in black and white.

During the war years and continuing up until his resignation in 1960, The Rt Rev. Christopher Chavasse was Bishop of Rochester.

This photo of an original painting by the celebrated portrait painter Sir Oswald Birley MC, RA dated 1938, hung in the St Andrew's vestry for many years.

The portrait was painted about two years before he became Bishop of Rochester. Both he and his twin brother Noel had distinguished military careers in the Great War.

Christopher was a military chaplain and earned a Military Cross and the Croix de Guerre amongst other awards. He was also awarded an OBE (Military Division).

His twin brother Noel Godfrey Chavasse, a medical officer with the rank of Captain, was the most highly decorated individual of the Great War, and was one of only three people to have been awarded the Victoria Cross twice (the second time posthumously).

Fig. 50 The Rt Rev. Christopher Chavasse
Photo: St Andrew's archives

Both brothers competed in the heats of the same event (400 metres) during the 1908 Olympic Games. Chavasse was the son of Francis James Chavasse (1846-1928) one-time Bishop of Liverpool who in retirement founded St Peter's Hall, Oxford, as a place where promising students of limited means could obtain an Oxford education. His son Christopher became the first Master in 1928, when there were only 40 students, and served for 10 years until shortly before he was consecrated bishop of Rochester. The hall eventually became a fully-fledged college of the University of Oxford. Both Christopher and his father were on the evangelical wing of the Anglican church. The original portrait to this day hangs behind high table in the Hall at St Peter's College, Oxford.

After Easter 1950, the Rev. S H Cooke left St Andrew's for a living in Somerset and in May of that year the Rev. W Trevor Rees was inducted and the vicarage at 23 Burnt Ash Lane was bought to replace the smaller house at the corner of Croft Road. The 21st anniversary of the church was celebrated in 1951. In 1956 Miss Molly Alchin, who had devoted many years of her life to supervising the Sunday School, resigned her post, which was then taken over by Mrs E Green.

Fr Rees served St Andrew's faithfully and became, at that time, the longest-serving incumbent, retiring after a term of fourteen years. Towards the end of 1964 ill-health forced his resignation and in June 1965 the Rev. P G L Cole came to St Andrew's on his return to this country from Rhodesia.

By 1966 the Assistant Clergy Fund had again reached a point at which, with the help of grants from the diocese and the Additional Curates Society and a generous offer by Mr Frank Stanger of a house in Hilldrop Road at a very favourable rent, the parish was able once again to have an assistant priest.

The Rev. and Mrs Adrian Vivian moved into the parish in April 1966 shortly before Adrian took up the curacy at St Andrew's. He had completed four years training at King's College, London, and St Boniface College, Warminster and was made Deacon by the Bishop of Rochester at Rochester Cathedral on 2nd October.

The first issue of the 'new-look' 'Burning Bush' - the parish newspaper of St Andrews - appeared in December 1965 and was distributed free to the 2,800 homes in the Parish.

Fig. 51   Rev. A J Vivian
Photo: St Andrew's archives

The Rev. D N Griffiths, who had been honorary curate at St Andrew's for two years, left the parish in September for a parish in Lincoln.

Fig. 52 Canon Peter Cole on a return visit to St Andrew's

In the autumn of 1967 under the guidance of the Rev. P G L Cole plans were prepared for Burnt Ash Housing Association Ltd to develop a scheme for 25 flatlets and a warden's flat on the vacant plot adjacent to the Church. The foundation stone was laid on 12th October, 1968 the ceremony being performed by the Rt Rev. H D Halsey, Bishop of Tonbridge. The vicar and several church members were active in the promotion and realisation of the scheme and it had the full support of the PCC, but the enterprise was representative of the whole community. It was on Saturday 13th September 1969, that St Andrew's House was opened by the Mayor of Bromley, Alderman G H Pratt, in the presence of Mr John Hunt, Member of Parliament for Bromley. The final cost was in the order of £110,000 almost entirely funded by a 60 year mortgage through the Borough of Bromley. The Friends of Burnt Ash Housing Association in addition raised over £600 to pay for other amenities not covered by the mortgage.

The St Andrew's Over 60s club celebrated its 21st birthday early in 1969. At that time club membership was 120. It was started in 1948 by Mrs E Ball who ran the club under the auspices of the WRVS for nine years before handing over to Mrs N Farris. Organisation of the club was in the hands of ten ladies who ran the regular Friday afternoon social meetings and the coach trips and group holidays.

In September 1969, Fr Ian Little joined the staff at St Andrews. A priest-worker, his full-time occupation being that of a quantity Surveyor, he was ordained Deacon in 1966 and priest in 1967. Before coming to St Andrew's, he served as honorary curate at St George's, Bickley for three years.

Mrs Daisy Standing, remembered for her sterling work at the Sunday school piano died in 1969.

On the departure of Rev. Adrian Vivian late in 1969, Rev. Colin Oxenforth came to St Andrew's from St Chad's College, Durham, where he took his degree and underwent his theological training.

Fig. 53 Rev Colin Oxenforth & Jane Coombes
Photo: Andrew Martin

84

His keen interest in the performing arts was to come to the fore during his ministry in the parish.

In May 1971 a committee was formed to co-ordinate work on making a new set of 250 kneelers for the church. The original five members were Mesdames Coombes, Hanner, Hodges, Stanger and Stubbs. Their work was to take several years, but the results have made an outstanding contribution to the church.

In 1970 plans were laid for members of St Andrew's to go on a pilgrimage to the Holy Land in the following year led by Fr Cole. Eighteen people made the trip in April 1971, of which eight were from St Andrew's. The 'Burning Bush', which had been re-kindled in 1965 had achieved a circulation of almost 1300 by 1970 and was priced 6d. The price had remained unaltered for five years with cost increases being covered by increased sales.

November 1970 saw the loss of one of the true stalwarts of St Andrew's. Frank Stanger lived almost his whole life at the same house at 17, Lake Avenue. He was secretary of the Building Committee in the late 1920s which was responsible for construction of the church. He was first secretary of the PCC, founder warden of St Andrew's Guild of Service and at various times Scoutmaster, Parish Treasurer and Churchwarden. Frank Stanger joined the army at 18, took part in both world wars, saw service abroad and during the Great War was wounded in both ankles and lost the sight of his right eye. After the war he was active in the British Legion and the Home Guard. He was a devoted servant of St Andrew's and an inspiration to many. In his multiplicity of activities he was staunchly supported by his wife Eileen, herself an active church member and daughter of an old Bromley family. Frank Stanger's generous bequest to the Church, augmented by numerous donations enabled the memorial window in the Lady Chapel to be planned early in 1971. The service of dedication was held in October 1971.

By April 1971 sufficient donations had been received to complete work on the East Window and the Bishop of Rochester came to dedicate it on 9th May. Known as the Te Deum window, it was designed by A K Nicholson, brother of Sir Charles Nicholson, architect of St Andrew's Church, and depicts the worship of God by all creation. There are eighteen panels. The centre row portrays God as Father, Son and Holy Spirit, the Christ Child, Our Lord on the Cross and Christ present at the Eucharist. The remaining panels each contain a figure or group of representative figures worshipping. The first three panels were put in during April 1935. The next three were added in 1954 and the remaining twelve between 1965 and 1971.

Thus the window took 36 years to complete. The last twelve cost between £70 and £100 each. The first six were installed by the A K Nicholson stained Glass studios and the last twelve by Luxford Studios of New Barnet. Apart from the five earliest panels and one (top centre) which was a gift from the young Wives Group, all have been given in memory of the departed. The service of dedication was attended by several former clergy of St Andrews, including Fr W T Rees, his predecessor Preb. S H Cooke, Canon R W Walls and by Mrs Griffiths, the widow of Rev. J M T Griffiths.

The massive task of making 250 tapestry kneelers had begun in the previous year and there was a display of the first completed examples at the church Annual Meeting in 1971.

May 1972 saw the departure of Rev. Peter Cole and his family after seven years of service to the parish. Fr Cole took up a post as Vicar of Folkestone and as a mark of appreciation a coach party from St Andrew's attended the induction service.

In the summer of 1972, after forty-two years 'existence, St Andrew's Guild of Service which had provided a focal point for so many young people of the church, ceased to meet. In the late Autumn of 1972, Fr Colin Oxenforth, who made a lively and enthusiastic contribution to the work of the church, moved to Peckham. Valerie Bucknall wrote of him 'We have enjoyed his clowning, and have laughed at his ridiculous remarks. Many of us have discovered that his good humour is founded on a very deep seriousness and understanding of people. We have found him willing to listen to our problems, regardless of his own. We have found that he really cares, and that means more than words can say.'

Fr Peter Hinchey brought with him his enduring love of music; in fact at one time he was heading for a career as a professional organist, but in 1955 he was accepted at Chichester Theological College for three years training for the Ministry. He was ordained in 1958, and St Andrew's was his fourth posting.

Mr Ronald Heald was awarded the MBE in the 1973 New Year's Honours List for his work in a leper colony at Lulindi. St Andrew's Guild of Service had for many years raised money to support a nurse at Mr Heald's hospital and he pad paid two visits to the Guild whilst on furlough and proved a fascinating speaker of great wit and warmth.

Towards the end of 1973 the Bishop of Rochester gave his permission for six laymen to assist with the administration of Holy Communion at 10.30 am service. Those who initially undertook this duty were Messrs Dalton, Hall, King, Perry, Wallace and Warner. In September 1974 Fr Ronald Cason was appointed Rector of

Stoke-on-Trent. Fr Cason is an old boy of St Andrews, born in 1928 and educated at Bromley County School (now Ravensbourne School). He was thoroughly involved in church life as a server, a member of the Guild and of St Andrew's Cricket Club (which later became Ravensbourne CC). On leaving school he went to Kelham Theological College until 1946 when he was drafted into the RAF. He was ordained deacon in 1953 and priest in 1954. At that time he was Curate at Fenton in the Potteries where he remained until 1956. He was Vicar of Brereton, Staffs, from 1956-63; Vicar of Hugglescote, Leics, from 1963-67 and became Vicar of Blakenhall Health, Walsall in 1967, remaining there until his appointment as Rector of Stoke-on-Trent in 1974. He described his main concern as a parish priest 'to build parish Communion-centred worship in the Catholic tradition; to encourage the young, for their own sake; to bring some discipline to bear upon the administration of baptism and to help where possible to defend human rights and dignities.' Fr Cason continued at Stoke and was appointed Rural Dean in 1978.

Fr Peter Hinchey inaugurated the Cellar Club for the young people of St Andrew's. They transformed the Vicarage cellar into a Sunday evening meeting room for talks, discussions and games, thus fulfilling a vital need in the parish. On 3rd November, 1974 St Andrew's wished God speed to the Hinchey family who moved to New Eltham where Fr Peter took up a teaching post.

Between Fr Hinchey's departure in November and the arrival of Fr Christopher Channer there was only a brief interregnum. Born in Walton-upon-Thames Fr Christopher was ordained in 1965 and served a three year curacy at St Stephen's, Norbury before moving to a further curacy in South Elmshall in the Diocese of Wakefield where he stayed until 1970. He then became Vicar of St Edmunds, Dartford, moving to St Andrews in January 1975. January 9th saw the church packed for his induction Present were the Bishop of Tonbridge, the Rural Dean of Bromley and clergy from neighbouring parishes plus a strong contingent from Fr Channer's Dartford parish.

Fig. 54 Rev. Christopher Channer at a church fête with Freda Hill
Photo: Andrew Martin

In 1975 Tony Taylor left after a two-year spell as organist and choirmaster to concentrate on composition. His place was taken by Alan and Sheila Knight.

A faithful member of St Andrews, who devoted much of her time and talents to the church, died on 29th July 1975. She was Bessie Bartholomew. For many years she had been Honorary Secretary and Warden of St Andrew's Guild of Service and had a great influence on the youth of the church.

She was a born organiser and was very active at the time the church was built. She wrote many songs, sketches and mock trials for entertainment and for the 21st anniversary of the church she prepared, after much research, a fascinating short history of the parish from 1885 to 1951.

Bessie's abiding love was for cricket; she was secretary of St Andrew's Cricket Club and was the club's regular umpire. Bessie was also a great enthusiast for the church garden. After her death a memorial fund was set up which enabled the church to build the brick wall across the frontage of the grounds together with the railings, posts, gates and new supports for the church notice boards. The building work was carried out with the assistance of a community service team and completion of the work greatly improved the west aspect of the church.

In 1976 Church Army Housing, a self-supporting daughter society of the Church Army, built the residential development in Burnt Ash Lane between 'The Teasel' (since demolished) and Kynaston Road.

Mr & Mrs Robin Hodges left the parish to live in Sutton in the summer of 1976. Both were faithful worshippers at St Andrews for many years and Robin was Head Sidesman. Mrs Hodges left behind the results of a true labour of love in the shape of 250 tapestry kneelers. The work begun in the time of Fr Cole and continued for several years paid for by individuals and from the proceeds of small fund-raising functions. Many members of the congregation worked kneelers to their own designs within the common edge pattern. The collection is thus unique. Many of the most richly coloured kneelers represent scenes from the Bible - the Three Kings, the lost sheep, the Nativity, Moses in the bulrushes and so on. Others depict Christian symbols such as the Chi Rho (a monogram of the first letters of the Greek Christos) the ship (representing the image of the church riding the storms) and the rose, a symbol of love, perfection and beauty. The fish was an early symbol of Christianity. Other kneeler designs represent organisations connected with the church. The beautiful bridal kneeler, worked in delicately pale colours, was by Mrs Shields.

A devoted and popular member of St Andrews, Bill Morris, died in August, 1976. He was a man of great good humour and splendid spirit who had contributed to the work of the church unstintingly for many years. It was he who braved many a frozen dawn to start up the coke fired boiler prior to early services in the days before oil-fired heating. He married in 1919 and came to Bromley in 1925. He was involved in concert party and charity work for many years where his specialities were ballads, comic songs and monologues. On arrival in Bromley from Walworth he founded the first youth club at the Valeswood Community Centre - the Downham Estate was then just being built. A keen gardener, he put in much work on the church grounds and a plaque in his memory stands to the right of the west door. Donations towards a memorial fund provided for shrubs and plants along the north wall and a flowering cherry near the west door.

Fr Frances Heydon began to assist with services at St Andrew's, having moved to Bromley College with his wife at Easter 1978.

A little bit of history was made at the Annual Vestry Meeting in March 1979 when Miss Eileen Clarke was elected the first lady churchwarden at St Andrew's.

10

The Golden Jubilee
of St Andrew's
1980

1980 marked the Jubilee of St Andrew's Church in commemoration of the day of consecration of the church by the Bishop of Rochester on 10th May, 1930.

Many events were planned by the vicar, Fr Channer, and the PCC. The first major event was a mission week in March led by three Franciscans, Brother Donald and Brother Victor from the Anglican Franciscan Community whose mother house is at Cerne Abbey in Dorset, and Sister Pauline of the female Franciscan order. A programme of services and associated events occupied a full eight days from Sunday 8th to Sunday 15th March.

Early in the year Rev. David Springthorpe, who was the second St Andrew's 'old boy' to be ordained (after Fr Ronald Cason), was appointed to his first living as Rector of Ash in Kent. As part of the Jubilee celebrations a Flower Festival was held over the weekend of 9th and 10th May. The event was enthusiastically supported and the church was a sea of colour for the Jubilee weekend. The service was attended by the Bishop of Rochester, Dr R D Say and by the Mayor and Mayoress of Bromley.

Several former St Andrew's incumbents were invited to preach at services throughout the year, the first was Preb. S H Cooke, present on the day of the Jubilee. After he left the parish in 1950 he spent the remainder of his career in the Diocese of Bath and Wells, first at Keinton Mandeville in Somerset, then at Long Ashton and finally at Compton Dundon from which parish he retired in 1976 to a cottage near Dulverton. He was appointed a Prebendary in 1964 and his activities included Diocesan Inspector of Schools from 1959 to 1973, and Diocesan Press Officer from 1971 to 1976. It was with sorrow that news of Preb. Cooke's death in June 1981 was received at St Andrew's. Fr Peter Cole returned to St Andrew's on 18th May. After leaving Bromley in 1972 he became Vicar of Folkestone. In the autumn of 1980 he was appointed an Honorary Canon of Canterbury Cathedral by

Archbishop Runcie. Whilst at Folkestone he chaired no fewer than ten organisations including the Council of Churches, Age Concern Kent County Partnership Forum and the governing bodies of two schools. He was also active in many other clubs and management committees.

After leaving Folkestone, in 1990 he was appointed Rural Dean of Alton, Hants. After an attempt to retire in 1992 the Bishop of Winchester appointed him Acting Rural Dean of Petworth for three years. In 2012 he is living with his wife Marian presiding over a family of five children and seven grand-children. Still actively taking services in local churches, weddings and funerals and now approaching 85, retirement still eludes him.

The third past-incumbent to visit the parish was Fr Peter Hinchey. It had been a sad blow when during his time at Bromley Fr Peter's wife Doreen was diagnosed as having multiple sclerosis and Fr Peter decided to give up parish work to become head of music first at a school in Stepney then at a girls' comprehensive school in Eltham. During these four years he helped out regularly at a church in Sidcup, but as Doreen's condition improved the decision was made to return to parish work. He became Vicar of All Saints, Footscray and retained his duties as Chairman of the Diocesan Church Music Committee, and as a Priest Associate of the Society of Retreat Conductors.

The fourth visitor was Fr W Trevor Rees. Still extremely spry in his eightieth year his return visit brought back memories of his great charm and dry humour.

The year also included a pilgrimage to Bayham Abbey following the 1980 visit to Walsingham. The Abbey, situated astride the Kent-Sussex border south of Tunbridge Wells, survived the destruction of the Reformation and is largely intact. The pilgrimage was organised by the Catholic Renewal Group in the Rochester Diocese and was led by the Bishop of Tonbridge.

The fifth former member of the St Andrew's clergy to return to the parish during 1980 was Fr Michael Dittmer who was curate between 1941 and 1943 during the incumbency of Fr Cooke. After leaving Bromley he moved to a Bristol parish. He was then responsible for four and sometimes six, Wiltshire village churches, including Castle Coombe.

Fr Dittmer's visit was followed in October by one from Fr Colin Oxenforth. After his spell at St Andrew's between 1969 and 1972, he became Curate at St Anthony's, Nunhead. He continued his preoccupation with social problems and one of his particular concerns was the housing shortage. It was his declared intention to go where the need was greatest. In November 1976 he moved to St Margaret's, Princes Road, Liverpool, where he was inducted as Vicar. This church is situated in one of the poorest, multi-racial inner-city districts. There his work with the needy and homeless continued.

The seventh and last visiting priest was Canon Raymond Walls, who came in November. From 1935 he had served as a deacon under the first vicar of St Andrew's, Rev. Martin Griffiths. In 1938 he moved to the church of St John the Divine, Selsdon, but in 1942 he was back at St Andrew's to take charge of the parish while Fr Cooke was serving as an RAF chaplain. Three years later he moved to St Peter's, Aylesford and then in 1946, he accepted a living in Suffolk, and served out the remaining thirty years of his ministry there. For the last eighteen of those years he was Rector of Ufford, and during his term in Suffolk he was chaplain to the County Psychiatric Hospitals, and held several diocesan posts. Although he officially retired in 1977 he was attached to St Dunstan's Canterbury, making his retirement somewhat illusory.

In December, 1980 Mrs Mary Raymer, a faithful member of the St Andrew's community, celebrated her 90th birthday. She was born on 7th December, 1890, at Greenwich in the Parish of St Alphege's Church, where she was baptised and where her father was a Churchwarden, and also where her husband served his first curacy. She was one of a family of nine children of whom two became priests. Her father, Richard Jackson, a lawyer, was at one time Mayor of Greenwich and Liberal MP for that borough. He was also a founder member of the London County Council in 1888.

Mrs Raymer was educated at the Roan School, Greenwich, and at St Catherine's School, near Guildford, after which she studied for her LRAM which she obtained when she was 19. She had learned to read at the age of four in order to be able to read to her younger brother William who was blind, and whose life story she later wrote. She also taught at the Sunday School and the King's Messengers.

When she was 20 she became engaged to the Rev. William Purser whilst he was home on leave from Burma where he had been working for six years as a missionary. Later that same year she set sail for Burma, where she was married, and joined Mr Purser in his work as Head of a Mission Station near Rangoon in the delta of the Irrawaddy, called St Michael's Mission, Kemendine.

One part of his work involved the training of Burmese and Karen clergy and he did a lot of translation work such as translating the Prayer Book into Karen. As very little work had been done for women Mrs Raymer started classes for them which subsequently became the first Mothers' Union in Burma. Some of her other activities were arranging women's conferences, writing stories for the King's Messengers' Magazine and playing the harmonium for services. She liked to recall that she took her first Burmese examination and had her first child when she was 21. She had five children, two boys and three girls, four of whom were born in Burma.

In 1914 she and her husband started a school for training and educating blind boys for whom no provision then existed. Her brother William, who was ordained in 1912, came out to Burma in 1918 to help with the work of the school, and there he stayed until he died in 1931. The fine work he did there has been commemorated by the memoir of his life which Mrs Raymer wrote and which was published by the Society for the Propagation of the Gospel (SPG), also by the little book for children called 'Blind Eagle'.

She was in Burma for 17 years with several home leaves during that time and has calculated that she travelled 64,000 miles by sea. On their return to this country Mr Purser had the living of Taynham for 12 years, and was subsequently Chaplain of Bromley College for seven years. Mr Purser died at the College in 1947. In 1951 she married a former Chaplain of the College, the Rev. Herbert Raymer, and they moved to Welbeck Avenue where they had four happy years together. Mrs Raymer was connected all her life with SPG and contributed after her retirement by collecting tinfoil, which raised over £750 for the work of medical missions

11

St Andrew's in the 1980s

Charles Clarke's untimely death occurred in March, 1981. His life had been inextricably linked with St Andrew's. He came to the church in 1931, the year after it was built, and he served as secretary and Warden of the Guild of Service, and as sidesman, Treasurer and Churchwarden. He had the unique distinction of serving with every Vicar of St Andrews up until the time he and his wife Ethel moved to Beckenham. He had been a tower of strength to all those incumbents who came to rely on his expertise. His many other interests included the Scout movement and the National Trust and the same excellence that he showed in his leisure-time activities was evident in his professional work, where his integrity was equally appreciated. It was for his work in the Government Actuary's Department, from which he retired as Directing Actuary after 45 years that he was awarded the CBE.

During the summer of 1981, Fr Christopher Channer who had served the parish faithfully since he moved to Bromley in January 1975 accepted the living of Langton Green near Tunbridge Wells. The parish said farewell to their sixth incumbent at a splendid gathering at the Church Hall on 6th September.

During the somewhat lengthy interregnum the reins were in the hands of the Churchwardens Leonard Rackham and Eileen Clarke. But the task of holding the church on course was made doubly difficult by the serious illness of Eileen. She died in December and great tribute was paid to her and the personal qualities she brought to her appointment as churchwarden. Not least was the bravery with which she faced her crippling illness. During the interregnum Fr Francis Heydon endeared himself to the people of St Andrew's as he came out of retirement at Bromley College to take the services until the new vicar was appointed. His achievement in delivering many a sermon full of wit and wisdom, without once being encumbered by so much as a single reference note, will be long remembered.

In February, 1982 the seventh vicar of St Andrew's was Instituted and Inducted. The Rev. Canon Gordon O'Laughlin came to the parish from the Diocese of York. He was born in Liverpool and in 1951 began his National Service in the RAF.

He was chosen to train as a Russian interpreter and went to the University of Cambridge to learn the language. In 1953 he went to Oxford and continued to read Russian for his degree. Three years later he began a two-year course to study for the priesthood at Wells Theological College and was ordained Deacon in 1958 at Winchester Cathedral to serve in the parish of St Francis of Assisi, Bournemouth. After a four-year spell there he established his connection with the Diocese of Rochester when he moved to St Barnabas, Tunbridge Wells.

In 1965 Canon Blanch (one-time Archbishop of York) invited him to join his staff at Rochester Theological College, where he was first Chaplain and later Sub-warden. At the end of 1969 he was appointed to be Vicar of St Alban's, Hull, a large suburban parish of 20,000 people. Fr O'Laughlin spent nine years there where, apart from parish work, his duties included training curates and looking after ordinands and junior clergy. Moving to York in 1977 he became a Canon and Prebendary of York Minster. After twenty-three years in the ministry Fr O'Laughlin was asked by the Bishop of Rochester to leave York and make his new home as Vicar of St Andrew's.

At the Annual Vestry meeting in March both Mr Leonard Rackham and Mr Cyril Wallace were re-elected, each for his fifth term of office as Churchwarden. Those elected to serve on the Parochial Church Council were Mr R Becconsall, Mrs D Bentley, Mr A Church, Mrs J Coombes, Mrs S Cox, Miss T Dulley (Hon. Secretary), Mr P A I Dulley, Mrs K Goodwin, Mr L Hanner (Hon. Treasurer), Mrs V Hughes, Mr A J Martin, Mrs E McFarlane, Mrs P Salmon, and Mrs J Smith. Mr M Hall and Mrs A King were re-elected as the representatives to the Deanery Synod.

12

Into the 21ˢᵗ Century

A SCRAPBOOK OF THE LAST 30 YEARS

Miss Thornton left Burnt Ash Infants School in the summer of 1982 after 31 years' devoted service. Up until the time she left, after her day at school, she regularly made tea for Miss Chester who herself taught for 35 years at the school and by 1982 was house-bound.

Harry Stubbs passed away in October 1982 after a long illness. Always a strong supporter of St. Andrew's he was proud to have been in the Grenadier Guards and had fought in the Great War

Under the guidance of Fr O'Laughlin the church was beautifully redecorated in 1983. On 3ʳᵈ July 1983 Rev. Neil Bunker was ordained Deacon and performed his duties at a Sung Eucharist of the same day. Former St. Andrew's vicar Canon Peter Cole and St. Andrew's 'old-boy' Rev. Preb. Ron Cason returned to the church for the Bishop's visit.

Fig. 55 Rev. Neil Bunker in 1984 on the day of his ordination with his father Sydney Bunker

In March 1984 Neil set up home at 56, Davidson Tower and throughout his almost 4-year spell at St. Andrew's did a great deal of pastoral work in and around the parish amongst the young, the deprived and the homeless.

Canon Gordon O'Laughlin celebrated his silver jubilee as an ordained priest in 1985.

Arthur Short died aged 81 in March 1984. He had been a staunch member of the congregation, having run the King's Messengers (later the Adventurers) and been a member of the Scout Parents and Supporters group. For many years he was the scenery builder for the drama group. He once made an impromptu cameo appearance when one of his upstage doors swung open during a performance while he was fixing some artifact to the rear wall. In recent years Arthur's shoes were filled with great distinction by Bert Howell. He and his team always seem to be able to create wonders on the postage stamp of a stage at St. Andrew's.

In 1985 Neil Bunker started a new ministry at the Farnborough Hospital Psychiatric Unit after recovering from a nasty accident on the football field when he broke his leg in two places. He always generously put this down to accidental causes rather than grievous bodily harm.

In December 1986 Fr O'Laughlin announced that he was to take up a new post at St. Patrick's Church, Brighton after a 4-year spell at St. Andrew's and in 1987 Neil Bunker, now with a full complement of legs, took up a full-time post as Chaplain to Farnborough and Orpington Hospitals.

Fig. 56 Rev. Tomás Creagh-Fuller(L), and friends

Photo: Andrew Martin

At a concert held at St. Andrew's in April 1987 it was announced by Tom Creagh-Fuller that a performance of Handel's *Messiah* would take place at the church on the following Good Friday under Tom as conductor. This inspired act of bravura marked the creation of one of the great supporters of local charities in the area. The concert raised funds for the Save the Children Fund and marked the inception of BOeS (Bromley Oecumenical Singers) which thrives to this day and has performed numerous concerts at home and overseas and raised many thousands of pounds for charity, Tom himself serving as chorus master for many years.

Rev. H. Anthony Atherton was Instituted and Inducted as vicar of St Andrew's on 30th October 1987. Anthony, with a degree in geology and a Diploma in Education, after his marriage to Veronica in 1968 became geologist to a river authority. He was sponsored for training for the ministry by the Bishop of St. Albans, trained at Westcott House, Cambridge and began his ministry at All Saints, Leamington in 1972. After a spell at Ramsden he became vicar of St. Mary's, Gravesend in 1978 where he stayed for nine years before coming to St. Andrew's.

The 60th anniversary of the laying of the foundation stone of the church was marked by a Eucharist on Sunday 30th July 1989 attended by Bishop Edward Holland and the Epistoller was Lord Cornwallis.

In May 1990 the Bishop of Rochester, The Rt. Revd. Michael Turnbull attended the service marking the Diamond Jubilee of the consecration of the church in 1930.

The 'Friends of St. Andrew's' was registered as a charity in 1991 with the aim of providing financial support to the church for the fabric of the church and hall and for improvements to the church grounds. The first project was the installation of a sound system for the church.

Fig. 57 Visit of the Bishop of Rochester to St Andrew's, May 2005
(L-R) Rev. H Anthony Atherton, Mrs Win Snell,
The Rt Revd Michael Nazir Ali   *Photo: Andrew Martin*

In June 1992 the area was hit by flash floods when 7 cm of rain fell in an afternoon. A tidal wave poured down some of the hills in the parish and several people were rescued from upper floors by boat. Several ground-floor flats at St. Andrew's House were affected

Fig. 58 Flash floods in Burnt Ash Lane   *Photo: Tony Isbitt Photography*

In May 1992 Jean Osborne became a licensed Reader at St. Andrew's. A new tabloid version of the *Burning Bush* was introduced which was circulated free to every house in the parish three time a year at Easter, Harvest and Christmas and this continues to the present day.

In 1992 St Andrew's lost one of its most active and well-loved figures when Cyril Wallace died. A fine Welsh bass singer, he had been a corner-stone in the choir established by Malcolm Warwick in the early sixties, then when the Dramatic Society was revived in 1961 he showed his artistic versatility by winning acting awards in the Bromley Drama Festival. Cyril was a tremendous raconteur with a splendid sense of humour. He served the parish church in various capacities including as Covenant Secretary, Missions Secretary and as Churchwarden.

In the same year the issue of admission of women to the priesthood in the Anglican church came to the fore and in November the General Synod took the momentous decision to admit women priests.

On 16th October 1992 Ethel Parham, a resident at St. Andrew's House and a regular member of St. Andrew's, celebrated her 100th birthday, sadly passing away the following year.

Due to a chance visit to the church in 1994, a link with wartime Bromley was established. Muriel Hinkley (née Thomas) now of Cove, Tiverton, Devon had lived at 43, Kynaston Road from 1931 until 1952. She remembered her early Sunday school days with Miss Beresford and Miss Alchin. She married Sub. Lieut. (A) S F Such at St. Andrew's but sadly he was killed in action in 1944 (see Ch 8). In 1952 she married Jack Hinkley who died in 1993 and it was to remember him that she came to the church in 1994.

In 1994 the church set aside the semi-circular garden at the front of the church as a Garden of Remembrance where the ashes of several people closely connected with the church have since been interred and a Book of Remembrance is kept in the church.

In June 1994 a great friend and supporter of the church died. Francis Heydon had trained at King's College, London. He was ordained Priest in 1937 and moved to St Peter Port, Guernsey where he assisted the Dean and was chaplain to the fort and the prison. When the island was about to be occupied in 1940 he wanted to stay with his congregation but had no choice but to change his plans when he discovered that as he was already in the RAF Volunteer Reserve he would be treated as a serving officer and sent to a POW camp. After the war he served as vicar of Holy Trinity, Paddington until 1962. He then moved to St Andrew's, Nuthurst, Sussex where he served as Rector until his retirement in 1978 when he became a resident of Bromley College. To the considerable benefit of St Andrew's, Bromley he became Honorary Curate and then acting Priest-in-charge during the interregnum between the appointments of Fr Channer and Fr O'Laughlin.

Fr Heydon will be long remembered with great affection by the people of St Andrew's for his true humility, the warmth of his personality and for his apparently effortless sermons, which were delivered unencumbered by so much as a single written note.

He died on 14th March 1994. He was prominent in the Freemasonry movement, holding office in the United Lodge of England, HRH The Duke of Kent being represented at his funeral at Nuthurst.

Fig. 59 Frank Chappell
Photo: Courtesy of USPG

Frank Chappell, another great servant of the church, died on 24th February 1995. Frank had served as Churchwarden in 1963 and in many capacities including as an altar server, as PCC Secretary and as auditor of the accounts. A chartered accountant, he will be particularly remembered for his decision to abandon a highly successful career in commerce to move to the Society for the Propagation of the Gospel (SPG) in 1960. He was a central figure in the arrangements to merge the SPG with the UMCA to become the USPG in 1965 from which he eventually retired in 1978. He also served with the Society of St Francis, setting up and administering the central fund.

Also in 1995 the parish lost Arthur Springthorpe, a true friend of St Andrew's. He was born in Greenwich, left school at 14 and was apprenticed as a motor mechanic. After the war he returned home to join the Ministry of Defence, gaining his qualifications at night school. Vehicle engineering was his abiding interest both professionally and as a hobby.

He and Gladys were married in 1936 at St George's Catford, immediately moving to Ridgeway Drive where they spent the whole of their long marriage, only just falling short of celebrating their Diamond Wedding anniversary. He was roundly upbraided by his father for paying the princely sum of £900 for the house, and when told that there was a plan to spend an additional £50 on a brick-built garage was virtually speechless.

Their sons Michael and David were both active in the parish and David became the second member of St Andrew's congregation to be ordained priest. Arthur was a member of the freemasonry movement and enjoyed many years of fellowship with his lodge in Croydon of which he was master in 1971/2 and through which was particularly active in support of St Christopher's Hospice, Sydenham.

May 1998 marked a momentous day in the annals of St Andrew's when Rev. Elizabeth Davis joined the staff as a non-stipendiary assistant priest. She had been a committed member of St Mary's, College Road, working as a Reader before becoming a Deacon and eventually being ordained Priest in 1994. Since 1998 she has made a very considerable contribution to the ministry at St Andrew's and is widely known throughout the area through various strands of her ministry.

The author's father Ken Martin died on 21st November 1998 and his mother Maude Martin on 31st August 2000. Both had served the church faithfully in various roles since moving to Thornton Road in 1939, then later to Lansdowne Road. Brought up in Catford, they married in 1939 at the outbreak of war. He served in the RAF at home, in India and the Far East, and after the war taught at Rangefield Road Primary School, Downham.

Ken Martin also ran a Club for the Blind on the Downham Estate, initially under the aegis of Toc H, but when the branch closed down, he carried on the work himself. Maud had to give up her post as private secretary to Sir Andrew Agnew at Anglo Saxon Petroleum (later Shell) in the days when to get married meant the end of a career. In the event she took on another full-time career bringing up her four charges.

In 1999 Evelyn Rackham died. Evelyn was a long-time faithful member of the St Andrew's congregation, and it was a generous bequest from her estate that gave hope that the money could eventually be found to re-build the church hall. In the autumn Joan Smith, of Sandringham Road, died. She had contributed to St Andrew's for many years through her membership on the Mothers' Union, serving on the PCC and starting the Parent & Toddler Club.

At the very end of 1999 Christopher Turner died. He and his wife Doris came to Bromley in 1934 and their son Bryan was born two years later. Father and son were members of the choir.

He was appointed Vicar's Warden in 1951, a post he held for 13 consecutive years until 1963. An accomplished, self-taught, organist, he gave regular assistance at St Andrew's until he and his wife retired to Birchington. Both he and his wife were dedicated church people.

Another loss to the local community occurred in 2000 when John Murray died. He had provided many local residents with dental services from his surgery in Headcorn Road, Downham over many years. He was man of great good humour and had the knack of being able to put the most nervous patient at ease.

His funeral Order of Ceremony aptly quoted from R G Ingersoll:

Happiness is the only good; the time to be happy is now; the place to be happy is here; the way to be happy is to make others so.

Nigel Green, Headmaster of Burnt Ash School left in 2001 after 26 years service and was replaced by Miss Janet Barrett.

Burnt Ash School Infant and Junior Schools are in 2012 combined into one school with one Head Teacher, currently Mrs Leah Crawley. The buildings are much the same, although the open-air corridors are now double glazed with better use of the internal space.

There are currently 416 pupils, including 19 pupils in the Special Opportunities Unit for moderate, severe and complex learning needs. Little Ashes Pre-School is attached to Burnt Ash School. The school is very popular with local people and since the "Greenwich ruling" in 1999, over 40% of the children live in the Borough of Lewisham rather than Bromley.

The intake at the school reflects the multi-cultural population of Downham, so many of the children do not have English as their first language.

The school is busy from 8am (breakfast club) until the evening with after-school clubs for football, cheerleading, judo, street dancing and music and many more activities! One of the internal courtyards is now a nature garden with a flock of chickens which provide the eggs for the breakfast club.

The school has active links with the local community and churches and took part in the Community Day to celebrate the Olympics. It also has links with overseas schools and often has overseas teachers visiting.

There is a Family and Children's Centre attached to the school as well, which offers classes in parenting, child development, baby clinic and language development to give confidence and help to local families.

On 22nd July 2001 the Bishop of Rochester Rt Rev. Michael Nazir Ali preached at the morning Eucharist and dealt with a lot of questions during the ensuing parish lunch in the church hall.

In May 2003 Leslie Smith died, three months short of his 100th birthday. He lived in Hilldrop Road and was to be seen cycling around the parish well into is 90s. He regularly attended weekday services at St Andrew's. Leslie worked for many years as a railway signalman and bought his house in Hilldrop Road when it was first built in 1926. Since then it has been in his family continuously. Leslie was immensely proud of his family and is pictured here with his grand-daughter Jackie Chambers, daughter of Jennie (née Smith) and Colin Chambers, who have lived for many years in Cape Town.

Fig. 60 Leslie Smith with granddaughter Jackie Chambers *Photo Courtesy Jenny Chambers*

In 2003 Angela King joined the staff as Deacon and on 26th June 2004 she was ordained Priest at Rochester Cathedral by the Bishop. Her first celebration of the Mass on the Sunday was followed by a celebration lunch at which she was presented with a portable Communion set. She immediately began her duties as Assistant Priest at St Andrew's.

May 2005 marked the 75th anniversary of the consecration of St Andrew's church and was celebrated with a week of events including an arts and crafts exhibition in the church, a Band Concert by the All Saints Concert Band, a fun-run, an open day, a children's day, a choral concert given by BOeS and a Celebration of Eucharist in the church with the Bishop of Rochester Rt Rev. Michael Nazir Ali as principal celebrant. The parish also welcomed Bishop Yohanna of Kondoh, Tanzania (a link diocese) together with his wife Mrs Dina Mkavu, and a delegation from the West Kent Freemasons and old friends with connections with St Andrew's.

In 2005 Rev. Elizabeth Davis was appointed to chair CTCB (Churches Together in Central Bromley) for a 3-year term from September 2005. She was also appointed Chaplain to the Mayor of Bromley, Cllr. Mrs Joan Wykes and a civic service to celebrate the Mayor of Bromley's year of office was held at St Andrew's on 17th July 2005.

An active and much-loved member of the congregation, Mabel Sharpe, died in 2005. Born in the East End, she qualified as a mechanical engineer in the days when that would have been an unusual profession for a woman. A keen photographer, she lived in Hilldrop Road for many years with her husband Lionel.

2007 marked the sad death of Marjorie Hrubes. Her husband Otto, a Czech national, who pre-deceased her, was an Auschwitz concentration camp survivor, who in common with many who survived terrible suffering in Nazi concentration camps, never spoke of his ordeal. He, remarkably, escaped from Auschwitz and made his way to England where he joined the RAF. After a whirlwind romance of three weeks in 1957 Marjorie and Otto married, living in Sandringham Road and later Kynaston Road, a happy marriage which lasted 44 years before Otto died. Marjorie was for a many years an active supporter of the Friends of St Andrew's.

In 2009 Lois Guinan-Brown died. She was a woman of indomitable spirit and a committed Christian. Rev. Colin Oxenforth returned to St. Andrew's to officiate at the funeral service. His memories of Lois were of a woman who came from an army family and had a compelling sense of duty. She had a full panoply of personal attributes but was a little light on tact. However all her many friends would have known that with Lois, provided you gave as good as you got, you would be fine. She was one of those characters whose departure left a larger than life-sized hole.

Also in 2009 we lost David Harrison, who in early life was brought up in the Burnt Ash 'village'. He sang in the church choir and was a member of the Guild of Service. He was also a keen athlete and cricketer. He always had a great love of the arts and music and in his professional life was an art director in the advertising business.

We said farewell to Fr Anthony Atherton on 26th September 2010 after his 23 years as vicar of St. Andrew's. Over the years he had championed several causes, not least Bromley Churches Housing Action (the 'LATCH' project), a charity created to assist homeless young people. He was a board member and chair of Penge Churches Housing Association which has 250 properties under its care. He was also a member of the Rochester Diocesan Board of Education for many years, for some time on the Burnt Ash School governing body and was a Governor of St Olave's School. He retired to Catford with his wife Veronica who had always staunchly supported him throughout his ministry.

2010 also saw the deaths of four long-time members of the St Andrew's congregation, Joyce Yea, Ellen Benoy, Win Snell (née Morris) and Graham Wallace, although Graham moved away from the parish to Petts Wood with his wife Linda and their family. Win had been a fixture at St. Andrew's having moved to Bromley from Walworth around 1929, the time St Andrew's was built. Apart from a spell living in Abbey Wood with her late husband Ernie, her entire life was centred around Burnt Ash, most recently living in Ridgeway Drive. In her early life she attended Burnt Ash School and during WW2 she was proud to have been appointed pick-axe monitor. It was her duty upon hearing an air-raid siren to ensure that she did not clamber into the air-raid shelter without her trusty pick-axe, in case they were faced with having to excavate their way out. An extremely generous bequest from Win's estate gave a tremendous boost to fund-raising for the hall re-building project.

Rev. Angela King was licensed as Priest-in-Charge by The Rt. Revd James Langstaff, the recently appointed Bishop of Rochester on 20th January 2011. The installation service was conducted by the Archdeacon of Bromley The Ven. Dr Paul Wright. Angela grew up in Cumbria, her father being an Anglican priest. Following a Post-Graduate Certificate of Education she taught English at Grey Coat Hospital, marrying Desmond and moving to Bromley where Desmond worked as a clinical psychologist at Farnborough Hospital. When the children were young she was on the Rochester Committee for the Ordination of Women (MOW) and started reading for a theology degree through Wolesley Hall. Angela was ordained deacon in 2003 and priest in 2004.

9th July 2011 saw the wedding of St Andrew's churchwarden Cllr. Michael Turner to Ms Janet McFarlane believed to be the first time that a serving churchwarden of St Andrew's has been joined in Holy Matrimony whilst in office.

Then in the following year there was another first for St Andrew's when Michael was elected Mayor of Bromley.

Over recent years the St Andrew's 'Pop In' has proved to be a very popular initiative, providing an opportunity for local people to meet informally at the church. The 'Pre-School' has thrived over many years under Lin Stimson, opening five mornings a week from 9.15 – 12.00.

2011 marked the passing of Win Ecott, a long-standing member of the St Andrew's community, widow of John Bertram Ecott who perished in the SS Lancastria disaster during World War II.

Fig. 61 John Malcolm Smith

Photo: Courtesy Jenny Chambers

On February 17th 2011 John Malcolm Smith died aged 78. He was a colourful character who lived his entire life at the same house in Hilldrop Road, where in later years he cared for his father who lived to the ripe old age of 99. He lived for music and for 30 years worked from the basement of Boosey & Hawkes, the music publisher, in Upper Regent Street. Such was his fame in the music business that he earned an obituary in the *Daily Telegraph* amongst other illustrious organs of the press. According to the newspaper there was rarely an evening when he was not to be found at a performance. He was in today's parlance a distinguished networker, and his opinions were widely sought and given.

He was also a fine sketch artist and on one occasion at dinner with Stravinsky, he produced a line drawing of the composer, which Stravinsky annotated with the words "I find this sketch very successful I. S.". This is reproduced opposite with the permission of the late John Smith's sister Jenny Chambers, now resident in Cape Town, who has deposited the original with the British Library. Malcolm was a contemporary of Bill Burford's at Bromley County Grammar School and saw service in the RAF in the 50s. He was a great champion of English music and belonged to the societies for Delius, Finzi, Elgar and Bantock.

He served as chairman of the LSO Club and was a member of the Royal Philharmonic Society. He also founded the Romeo (Retired Old Men Eating Out) Group, which sprang from his retirement party, itself an alcoholic legend in the music industry, which was attended by Oleg Prokofiev, Ursula Vaughan Williams, Tasmin Little, Jane Glover, Lady Groves, Edward Downes and David Lloyd Jones. For his 65th birthday, the composer Robin Holloway composed a piece of music and Malcolm Smith left a legacy to fund its recording.

Igor Stravinsky
25th June 1964

Fig. 62 John Malcolm Smith's sketch of Igor Stravinsky, drawn on the back of a restaurant menu, 1964.
Reproduced by kind permission of Jenny Chambers (née Smith), sister of John Malcolm Smith

After a long gap with no regular choir leader, in 2011 Gloria Toplis became organist and choir-mistress at St Andrew's, bringing a new and welcome level of enthusiasm for choir activities.

Fig. 63 St Andrew's Choir and clergy 2012
From the left,

Back row: Andrew Martin; Thelma Dulley, Bob Kinnear, Rev. Angela King, Rev. Liz Davis, Peter Dulley.

Front row: Ann-Marie Martin, Andrea Gambell, Carolyn Hunt, Daphne Williams, Gloria Toplis, Nanetta Justice, Laurie Williams

Photo: Ivan Nenov

In August 2012 Malcolm Hall died. He was born in 1928 in Deptford to William and Jessica Hall. He went regularly to St Paul's Church Deptford with his aunts until World War II when he was evacuated firstly to Fairlight then Narbeth, Wales. After the war he returned to London to study and work as a book-keeper and accountant. He married Alice Codling in 1956 at St Andrew's, her parish church. They moved to Bromley in 1957, first to Burnt Ash Lane then, following the birth of their daughter Deborah, to Ridgeway Drive. He worked as an accountant and eventually as finance director of Foster Electrical Supplies, a subsidiary of Thorn EMI from the late '60s until his first retirement in 1987. After Alice died, he joined the Diocese of Gibraltar-in-Europe as the Finance Secretary. Shortly after his second retirement in 1994 the diocese formed a Friends Committee and he was asked to serve on it as Gift Aid Secretary and then Secretary until his final retirement.

A former churchwarden of St Andrew's, he was honoured by HM the Queen, receiving the Maundy Money on the occasion of the Queen's 85th birthday. Malcolm served on the staff of the Diocese of Europe for 22 years. He continued to be active in Freemasonry up until his death as well as at St George's Church, Bickley where he served and represented the parish on the Deanery Synod.

At Harvest Festival in 2012 Rt Rev. Dr Brian Castle, Bishop of Tonbridge visited the parish. After the service, the Scouts took a trek-cart full of donations of food to the Orpington & Bromley Food Bank.

Fig. 64 (L-R) Rev. E Davis, Rev. A King,
Janet Mayberry, Bishop of Tonbridge
Photos: Andrew Martin

Fig. 65 Harvest Festival 2012.
Back row (L-R) John Povey (Scout Leader),
Adam Panizzi (Explorers Leader),
Emma Povey (Cub Leader), Rev Angela King,
Mary Beckingham, Bishop Brian of Tonbridge,
Front row L-R) Ben Hickman, Samuel
Rogers, Nathan Ficalho

Fig. 66 Visit of Bishop of Tonbridge to
St Andrew's, October 2012. L-R Michael
Turner, Churchwarden and Mayor of
Bromley, Janet Turner, Lady-Mayoress,
Rt Rev. Dr Brian Castle, Bishop of
Tonbridge, Nanetta Justice, Derek
Justice, Churchwarden

Fig. 67 Rev. E Davis and Rev. A King
2012

St Andrew's parish is fortunate to have such a wide variety of local shops on the Sundridge Parade. Three of the longest established businesses are featured below.

Tony Isbitt Photography

Fig. 68 Minns General Store on the Sundridge Parade run since 1961 by the Silverthorne family.
From left: Steve, Marie, Robert and Lynn Silverthorne

Photo: Andrew Martin

(L-R) Colin Bristow, Tony Isbitt, Alan Hunter

Photo: Tony Isbitt Photography

Three generations of J Andrews, Family Butchers on the Sundridge Parade since 1948
Fig. 70 from left: John, Ellen, John Snr and Ray Andrews
Fig. 71 John and son Johnny Andrews

The parish contains over 2,800 households and there are few vacant plots of building land left. Many of the large Victorian houses have been demolished to be replaced by smaller modern homes. But despite the intensive housing development of recent years, the parish is still bordered by a most beautiful stretch of open countryside; the Sundridge Park Golf Course and the wooded grounds of the Sundridge Manor Hotel. King's Meadow and the Westminster School playing fields provide two small lungs amid the urban sprawl, and if you did but know it, a climb to the top of the reservoir above Thornton Road on a clear day provides a view right across London to Hampstead Heath to the northwest and to Shooters Hill to the north. Many of the famous London landmarks can easily be picked out.

Over recent years much work has been done to plan the long-overdue rebuilding of St Andrew's Hall. Despite the daunting nature of the task, at the time of writing, the target is within sight, thanks to the determined efforts of members of the congregation over many years and several generous bequests from former church members.

The area continues to be tied rigidly to the Great City, and extensive new commercial office development in Bromley is unlikely to loosen the knot.

We have certainly come a long way since Monsieur Guines came over with the Conqueror and settled on Sundridge as a pleasant spot to set up his country seat. I wonder what he would make of it now!

13

900 Years Ago

In his research into the history of the parish of St Andrew's, the author was fortunate to unearth one of the early issues of the 'Burning Bush'. The copy was dated July 1082 and the original vellum was in a good state of preservation. In those days the 'Burning Bush' was a substantial scroll telling of the doings at St Andrew's, then a wattle and-daub chapel standing atop Powsty's Hill by the ducking pond.

There was evidently a superfluity of naughtiness about as the Kalendar for the month alludes to twice weekly ducking sessions. In his notes for July the vicar complained that once again he was having to chastise certain serfs for participating in all night wode parties. On the domestic side the ladies of the hamlet were congratulated on their splendid thistle and ragwort arrangements and the churchwardens listed those on the rota for scything the burial mound.

The Maters' Union announced a 'Bring and Barter' sale and the Youthe Clubbe their regular quarterly hike to the Hardicanute's Head, Hollow Bottom 'for the supping of olde ale'. Godric Erchenbaldus, reviewing the Burndish Strolling Players production of 'I was Eadwig's Butler' complained that he would have enjoyed the production a great deal more if 'sparks' had been able to keep the cressets going long enough for him to have seen the last act. As it was he had stubbed his toe leaving the auditorium and went to bed in a mighty rage. In the choir notes the Master of the Musick warmly welcomed two treble rebec improvers but regretted that the leading sackbut player had failed to turn up to rehearsal two Wednesdays running. He hoped that rumours that the player had defected to Farwig were unfounded.

The editor, one Willielmus de Burgered, drew attention to the difficulty caused by contributors delivering their material for the 'Burning Bush' verbally. Whilst this was all right for handing down legends, he would prefer copy to be handed in on vellum in crabbit Latin.

This was altogether a fascinating account of St Andrew's just after the Conquest. Whether it will form the basis of a truly comprehensive history of the parish, only time will tell.

14
Appreciations

Having had a life-long fascination with obituaries, probably because they show how much some people managed to cram into one short life-span, I ask for your indulgence with a small handful of 'appreciations' of local people who fall comfortably into that category.

Adelaide Woodforde-Booth and Capt. C V Woodforde-Booth M C

Fig. 72   Adelaide and Capt. C V 'Pat'
Woodforde-Booth M C (about 1950)
Photo: Courtesy Penny Reid
(née Woodforde-Booth)

In March 2006 Adelaide Woodforde-Booth died at the age of 93. She lived quietly in Thornton Road after she was widowed in the 1970s. She had a fascinating family history.

Her mother Marcella Jarvis, was a direct descendant of William Penn. Marcella herself was a remarkable woman, who when told by her doctor that she would not survive another winter in the inclement weather of New York and that she must repair to somewhere more congenial like California, was so horrified by the idea that she searched the atlas for another place with a similar climate, and the pin was stuck in the map at Santiago, Chile. Marcella married Filidomo Ramos and in Chile her family thrived. She spent much of her life caring for the poorest of the poor, the street children of Santiago, personally giving them an elementary education and a measure of stability in their young lives.

Adelaide met 'Pat' her future husband, during the second World War. Pat, Capt. C V Woodforde-Booth M C, at the time had been posted by the Foreign Office to Punta Arenas, the most southerly city in the world. Adelaide was in the middle of an adventure and arrived there on a tramp steamer as the only female passenger. The meeting and subsequent events leading to their marriage is the stuff of a separate romantic novel. Not least the story of how she was in such a rush to get on the returning boat that, having no pencil, wrote out her address for him in lipstick before running up the gang-plank. Eventually they got married by proxy in Uruguay with her husband thousands of miles away within hailing distance of Cape Horn.

Pat had served with the Border Regiment attached to the 45th Bn Royal Fusiliers which was part of the North Russia Relief Force which was posted to Russia to fight immediately after WW1. His M C was Gazetted on 3rd February 1920.

At that time he was named Charles Vincent Booth and changed his name by deed-poll in July 1920, adding his mother's maiden name, apparently to distinguish him from the plethora of military Booths.

Pat, over the years following his retirement from the army in 1927 had various consular postings, including to Punta Arenas, Chile (1939), Antofagasta, Chile (1946), Curacao, Netherlands Antilles, off the coast of Venezuela (1948) and Kobe, Japan around 1950. Adelaide first came to UK in 1945, as Pat's wife, returning several times and eventually arrived to settle here, by then with a small addition to the family, her daughter Penelope.

Adelaide was like a fish out of water, having been used to the little luxuries which came with diplomatic status and for some months lived out of a suitcase in London hotel rooms. One day she put her foot down and informed Pat that she had no intention of bringing up her little daughter in such conditions and she needed a house. Pat had a considerable military bearing and was probably unaccustomed to finding himself under orders. Nevertheless he took her request to heart. Not being the sort of man to go house-hunting, he gave Adelaide a budget and, who knows, some marching orders. She finally found No. 13 Thornton Road and suggested he took a look. Being short of time that day he declined and bought it sight unseen.

She told the story of the day she arrived in a cold house without a stick of furniture. The author's father, living at number 11, took round a tray of tea and biscuits and introduced himself. He immediately realized that there was a cultural gap to fill in that running a house was not something that either Pat or Adelaide had ever had to do and offered to light the coke boiler for her. 'Boiler' she said, à la Edith Evans, '*what* is a boiler'. They soon learned the ropes and settled in.

Adelaide was highly intelligent and extremely well read. In her library was a book *The Uttermost Part of the Earth* by E. Lucas Bridges which is a quite remarkable story of the earliest colonization of that fascinating part of S. America, the Tierra del Fuego. Adelaide knew personally several of the characters in that book and could name the individuals who sat round the dinner table at some remote spot 60 or 70 years previously. She had a great talent for quietly encouraging and nurturing the young who happened to cross her path.

That, beyond doubt, is something she inherited from her own mother who had given hope to those deprived street kids in Santiago a century before.

Professor Frank Spooner

Another fascinating character who also lived not a mile from Milk Street, in Chatsworth Avenue, was Professor Frank Spooner who died in June 2007 at the age of 83. He lived a life of unquestioned academic brilliance gaining his first doctorate at the age of 28. He went on to attain three professorships, at Chicago, Durham and Paris plus eight or nine doctorates.

He produced published works in his own chosen field of economic history in several languages. He never forgot he had been born in Australia. His teacher upbraided him for the use of the word 'fortnight' no doubt, because she thought it un-Australian. All that finished when, at the age of nine, he returned to Britain.

Fig. 73 Close-up from Fig. 74

During the Second World War he served as a volunteer sub-lieutenant in the Wavy Navy, 'an officer qualified in visual signals and Wireless/Telegraphy'.

He served in a variety of ships from minesweepers to flotilla-leader cruisers. He once spoke of the frisson he had experienced in the Far East when the first kamikaze came over the horizon.

In 1946 he returned to Cambridge to complete a wartime two-year 'short' degree, having seen both Nagasaki and Hiroshima and having been present at the reopening of the Tokyo British Consulate, resplendent in tropical whites and sword-belt.

Fig. 74 Christ's College, Cambridge 1942 *With the assistance of Christ's College, Cambridge Alumni Office, as far as it is possible to ascertain, this photograph taken in 1942 shows Frank Spooner 2nd from the left in the 2nd row from the top.* Photo: *Courtesy Christ's College, Cambridge*

A life-time bachelor, although once commenting that there were a couple of near-misses, he was genial and perceptive with a delightful sense of humour. He was a brilliant lecturer, always without notes. Ian Trenowden who gave his tribute at Frank's funeral on 6th July 2007, to whom the author is indebted for the above notes, concluded by saying that 'he lived respected and died regretted'.

He was an old boy of Bromley Grammar School (now Ravensbourne School) and must surely have amassed the most impressive panoply of qualifications of any student of that seat of learning. The list reads as follows:-

Christ's College, University of Cambridge (Hist. Tripos, 1st Cl., Ptl 1947 and Pt II 1948; MA 1949; PhD 1953; LittD 1985)

1948: Bachelor Research Scholar;

1949-1950: Chargé de Recherches, CNRS, Paris;

1951: Allen Scholar;

1951-1957: Fellow, Christ's College, Cambridge;

1955-1957: Commonwealth Fund Fellow, at Chicago, Colombia, New York and Harvard Universities;

1957-1961: Ecole Pratique des Hautes Etudes, VI Section, Sorbonne;

1958-1959: Lecturer, University of Oxford;

1961-1962: Visiting Lecturer in Economics, Harvard University;

1962-1963: Irving Fisher Research Professor of Economics, Yale University;

1963-1964: University of Durham: Lecturer then Reader;

1965-1970: Resident Tutor-in-Charge, Lumley Castle;

1966-1985: Professor of Economic History, University of Durham, later Emeritus;

1969-1976: Director, Institute of European Studies;

1976-1978: Leverhulme Fellow;

1985-1986: Leverhulme Emeritus Fellow;

1970: FRHistS ;
1983: FSA;
1957: Prix Limantour de l'Achadémie des Sciences Morales et Politiques;
1979: West European Award, British Academy;
1983: Ernst Meyer Award
 amongst other academic activities.

Only a few months before he died he kindly agreed to chair 'The Friends of St. Andrew's' and did so enthusiastically until shortly before his death.

Bill Burford

Bill Burford edited the first edition of *Not a Mile from Milk Street* when it was first published in 1982. He died on 11th February 2006. He was a highly intelligent, articulate and cultured friend to many at St. Andrew's and elsewhere.

In his early years he was active as a member of St. Andrew's Guild of Service and as a Sunday-school teacher. One of his consuming interests was drama and he was a leading light in the reformation of St. Andrew's Dramatic Society in 1961 (which became BADA in 1975) of which he was founding chairman. Bill was instrumental not only in striving for the highest performance standards but in tackling serious drama to great effect on the tiny stage of St. Andrew's hall.

Fig. 75 Bill Burford
Photo: Courtesy Doris Burford

It was rare that he was not either treading the boards or directing productions. From 1978 he also took the group several times to the open-air cliff-top Minack Theatre at Porthcurno, Cornwall for ambitious and successful productions.

He helped to carry away the silverware in the Bromley Full-Length Drama Festival and in reaching the finals of the Kent Festival. He also worked with Whitfield Players and took part in the ground-breaking Mystery Play cycles staged by the combined churches in Bromley in the '60s.

He had an abiding love of orchestral and choral music which found expression during the period of his membership of St. Andrew's choir which dated back to the days of Herbert Woodhams and Malcolm Warwick. His rich natural baritone voice was of the highest quality.

He spent much of his spell of National Service in Germany where he acquired a liking for all things German, to such an extent that he could never be persuaded to spend any time in France.

His sporting prowess was evident at St. Andrew's CC (later Ravensbourne CC). Legend has it that he produced some of the most alarming leg-break bowling ever seen in the South-East.

He developed an unlikely fascination for the Zulu wars and visited South Africa in pursuit of this interest.

Bill had a life-long love of the English language. This was exemplified in his professional life where he was never far from a need for the use of immaculate grammar, spelling and syntax. In his long spell at Church House, many was the time he had to wrestle with an abstruse, well-meaning draft report containing long sentences lacking the luxury of a verb. However poor the raw material, by the time the report was published, he would have ensured that the end result made perfect sense.

For many years he used his considerable literary skills to edit the Burning Bush. During his eventful life, Bill had many triumphs. One such was learning to drive. Although incredibly mentally dexterous Bill was never one for anything mechanical, so it was a considerable surprise when he passed the test. In an utterly selfless gesture, having proved he could pass, he never again got behind the wheel of a car.

The thing that perhaps defined him best was his acute sense of humour which was very much on the dry side. Bill was always suspicious of the Exchange of the Peace, and he was not above slipping out of church for a quiet drag on his pipe when the Peace loomed. The author on one occasion was sitting next to him when the Peace was announced. He looked across at him and, completely dead-pan, said 'If I don't hear from you by 11 o'clock, a state of war will exist between us'.

Bill Burford was a complex and intensely private man who did not always get the breaks he deserved, but he will surely be remembered as a man with a great sense of both duty and humour and as a true, loyal and generous-hearted friend.

Bessie Bartholomew

Bessie's contribution to the history of the Burnt Ash area was considerable, but aside from her other talents, she was a poet of no inconsiderable ability. Some of her work won poetry prices. I would like her to have the last word, of special interest to the 21st century residents of Kynaston, Sandringham, Thornton and Powster Roads, and over Powster's Hill via Hillcrest Road, tumbling down to the brook in Shaftesbury Park. What Bessie so eloquently brings to life can be seen on the cover of this little volume, photographed by the late S.P. Webber.

Before Downham Was

I wonder – did the moist brown earth below
Know when it lost its green and living skin
And feel the weight of solid brick and stone
Restraining and imprisoning it within?

This little brook once wandered as it chose,
With trilling larks above its grassy flanks;
Now, rubbish-laden, silently it goes,
Straight-jacketed between its concrete banks.

Amid the brick and steel of man's design
This fragment of a hawthorn hedge lives still –
I close my eyes and see its whole green length
Dividing Withycombe's and Powster's Hill

Ah, Powster's Hill, whose wiry, sheep-cropped turf
Was the whole world to us in childhood days,
Whereon we picnicked, blackberried, climbed trees,
Toboganned, searched for nests, learned nature's ways

I wonder – do you mourn for that green garb
In which for countless ages you were dressed?
Or are you unaware of outward change –
Am I alone bereft and dispossessed?

Bessie Bartholomew

Appendix I
Organisations

St Andrew's church has for over eighty years provided a focal point not only of the Christian faith, but as a centre of social activity. Numerous organisations have flourished over the years; some have come and gone and others have stood the test of time. The notes which follow give brief histories of groups and organizations which have been active in the Burnt Ash area.

The Mothers' Union

The Mothers' Union at St Andrew's was started by Mrs Amy Chater on 21st March, 1933. Mrs Chater was a much loved and very active person in church. It was due to her keen interest in the Mothers' Union that she was asked by the first vicar, the Rev. J M T Griffiths, to form a branch in the new parish. The official opening was on 21st March, 1933. At first the meetings were held alternately with the Mother Church Branch at St Mary's, Plaistow, but early in 1936 it was decided to stand alone. Mrs Chater also started a 'Woman's Hour' on Monday afternoons for any women with young children to get them away from the washing.

Mrs Chater was one of the moving spirits at the war Hospital Supply Depot during the last war. She was a great worker for Alexandra Rose Day. She died at the age of 79 on 15th June 1942 as a result of an accident in April. In 1939 Mrs Gilpin became Enrolling Member and held the office for nine years. There was a strict rule that Sunday best hat and coat were required attire for meetings, and the Enrolling Member was not above disciplining members for failing to meet the required standard of dress whilst in church. The third Enrolling Member was Mrs Rees, the vicar's wife, served for six years and Mrs Martin took over from her in 1956 until 1958. The Prayer Group was transferred to the Church and continued to meet until about 1973.

Every year there was an Overseas Sale either in Mary Sumner House or Church House, Westminster, where gifts from members in different parts of the world were sold, the proceeds going to the Overseas work of the Mothers' Union.

In 1959 Mrs Clarke became the Enrolling Member and remained until 1967. During her period in office a link was established with Jane Furze Hospital in Pretoria and a link in Australia. Members took turns in answering correspondence. There were about thirty members at this time and every three years there was a coach outing to Rochester Cathedral and tea afterwards at the old Corn Exchange.

Incidentally, Mrs Clarke formed a Young Wives Group in 1949. Its purpose was to encourage younger mothers to join the Mothers' Union and it was affiliated to the Mothers' Union. Mrs Grace Bardouleau was Enrolling Member from 1967 to 1973 when ill health forced her to resign. She was an Indoor Prayer Circle Member for five years until she died in June 1981. Mrs Joan Smith was appointed then by the vicar, Fr Hinchey, in 1973 and served for seven years. In the same year a new Charter was drawn up which caused much controversy in the movement, and as a result of which many members of the Mothers' Union resigned. Mrs K Goodwin had only been a member for a year when she became Enrolling Member and she held the office in 1982. The longest serving members of the group at that time were Mrs Talbot who was admitted on 10th February, 1942 end Mrs Sprules who joined on 5th August, 1940.

St Andrew's Women's Guild
(Formerly St Andrew's Young Wives Open Group)

The first meeting of the group was held on the last Tuesday of October 1949 in the home of Mrs Ethel Clark at 165 Burnt Ash Lane. Mrs Glaisyer, the wife of Canon Hugh Glaisyer of Bickley, came to inaugurate the Group. Mrs Clarke was Chairman and Secretary and Mrs Vera White was Treasurer. Eventually membership increased and the Group transferred to the Hall for their meetings, although they still meet once a month for a Coffee Evening in a member's house.

Their varied programme covered topics ranging from the work of an Anglican Nun, slides on travel, what to do in a nuclear attack, St Christopher's Hospice, the life of a London cabbie, antiques, guide dogs for the blind and Chelsea pensioners, to cookery demonstrations, flower arranging and keep fit. Some excellent speakers addressed their meetings including the then Rev. W Fenton Morley, later Canon, then Dean of Salisbury Cathedral, and Rev. Chad Varah who formed the Samaritans, and his wife who later became Central President of the Mothers' Union. The programme also included visits to the Ideal Home Exhibition, a bakery, Bromley telephone exchange, the Evening News and Standard, and a tour of Inns of London. In October 1970 the Group celebrated its 21st birthday with a party. Mrs Barbara Coles was leader at that time and many former leaders and members attended. Among them were Mrs Clarke, Mrs Nicholson, Mrs Edwards, Mrs Robinson, Mrs Harrison and Mrs Benton.

The Group ran a stall at both the Summer Fête and the Christmas Market. In addition they prepared the Easter Garden and decorated the church Christmas tree. They also contributed towards the top centre panel of the East Window of the church. In the 1960s the Group began to support Josephine, a Madagascan girl, and paid for her education on the mainland. She has now left school and the Group was asked if it would send funds for the Mission School at Tamatawe in Madagascar and this the Group continued to do. At the 1981 AGM it was decided that the name of the group should be changed to encompass all ladies, not just young married ones, and obtained Fr O'Laughlin's blessing in March 1982 when the new title of St Andrew's Women's Guild was adopted.

The group is still going strong in 2012. A full programme of talks and activities has included speakers on child minding, Martin Luther's Germany, anecdotes of an actor, and British Music Hall and Variety, the work being done by the Royal Mission to Deep Sea Fishermen and Mercy Ships. Other subjects covered included the Central Royal Parks, on being the son of a tea taster, the fun of recycling, and hairdressing and beauty.

The Guild's deputy leader, Veronica Loh, told the story of Canadians at Orpington Hospital in WW1. Social evenings comprised a quiz devised by Vivienne Avis, a poetry evening for Valentine's day organised by Pat Wilson and a very popular evening spent playing parlour games. The New Year party and the summer social were well attended as was the Christmas lunch at the Bromley Court Hotel. The summer outing to Hall Place took place on the hottest day of the year, but was enjoyed by those who made the effort.

The Group holds an annual Carol Service supported by Bromley Oecumenical Singers and supports St Andrew's Church by running stalls at the Summer Fair and Christmas Market. It regularly donates money raised by the coffee evenings in members' homes, to the Friends of St Andrew's and supports the rebuilding of St Andrew's Community Hall.

The former secretary of the Group, Pat Favargue arranged a varied and stimulating programme of talks over the years. Despite crises, such as speakers not turning up and, on one occasion, two arriving on the same evening, she remained calm and unflappable. A newcomer to the committee, Veronica Loh served as deputy leader and became secretary.

St Andrew's Guild of Service

St Andrew's Guild of Service, formed in 1930 was a unique organisation. It was not a youth club, full membership being restricted to young communicant members of the Church, but somehow meant a great deal more to its members that the average youth fellowship. The objectives of the Guild were to inspire the Spirit of Service, to co-operate with the Vicar and PCC in carrying out Church work and to promote social intercourse, mutual helpfulness and the ideals of Christian fellowship.

The origins of the Guild can be traced to a Parochial Church Council meeting which took place on 3rd December, 1929. The idea was to form a Guild to give young people a greater interest in the activities of the church and who would be ready to undertake any work which might be necessary.

Those deputed to develop the idea were Miss Beresford, Mrs Wise, Mrs Lawdon-Eaton, Mr Sherriff, Mr Sheldon and Mr Stanger. Leading lights in the early days were Frank Stanger and Charles Clarke. By the early forties a tradition had been established of regular bank holiday Guild 'hikes' designed to combat even the most serious after-effects of festive over-indulgence. Each year the Guild took the presents donated at the children's toy service to one of several East London churches from where they were distributed to underprivileged children in the area.

Fig. 76 St Andrew's Guild of Service 1948

From left:

Back Row: 1 Derek Dickins, 2 Bryan (?), 3 Peter (?), 6 Gladys Bateman, 7 Gerald Freek, 8 Eileen Wright, 9 David Manning, 10 John Field, 11 Peter (?), 12 Alan Short, 13 David Harrison, 15 Jimmy Thomas

Middle Row: 16 Ron Gilbert, 17 Ray Ireland, 18 Bessie Bartholomew, 19 Rev S H Cook, 20 Charles Clarke, 21 Win Morris, 22 Bill Burford,

Front Row: 23 Joan Lewington, 24 Doris Burford, 25 Doris Green, 26 Betty Jerome, 27 Pam (?), 28 Cynthia Talbot, 29 Pam Blake, 30 Rita Talbot

During the war Guild members serving overseas were kept supplied with knitted clothes and food parcels. Although Guild minute books prior to 1955 have unfortunately gone astray, the parish magazine for March 1940 records that the first meeting of the Guild was held on 13th January, 1930. One of the more perilous tasks undertaken by the Guild was repainting the flag-staff. Even during the war with many young men members in the services, monthly meetings attracted an attendance of forty or fifty members.

Programmes included group discussions, talks by outside speakers, brains trusts, dances, social functions and innumerable odd jobs connected with the church. The Guild also frequently supported the functions of the Deanery Youth Committee. The Guild had some lean years and many a good year but shortly after the departure of Fr Cole in 1972 it ceased to meet after having survived for forty-two years.

25th Bromley Scout Group

The history of the Group dates back to July 1930 when the application was made to form a Scout Group at St Andrew's. The '25th' was registered with Imperial Headquarters on 8th August, 1930, sponsored by the first vicar of St Andrew's, Rev. J M T Griffiths, with twelve Wolf Cubs under Assistant Cub-Masters John Gayford and Roger Ackerley.

Mr Frank Stanger formed the Scout Troop in 1937 and from 1941- 1946 the Group combined with the 14th Bromley owing to the absence of Officers during the war, and were led by Acting Scoutmaster Alan Day and Troop Leader Douglas Hamon.

In 1947 the Troop returned to St Andrews and Mr Arthur 'Skip' Field took over as Group Scout Master. The Field Family played a great part in scouting at St Andrew's and many ex-scouts had happy memories of the 'Gang Shows'. In 1958 Mike Gathergood became Scoutmaster and Mr Field became the Chairman of the Parents' and Friends' Association.

In 1961 Mike Gathergood resigned and Malcolm Stewart took over as Scoutmaster and in 1968 the leadership passed to Wayne Bowman, a New Zealander who was working in this country. On his return to New Zealand in 1969 the leadership passed to Ken Ridgway.

In 1972 the Group was re-formed under the new scheme of Group Executive and Group Council. It was equipped with new tents at a cost of £700. Since that time the Group has maintained its strength and position in the Scout District of Bromley. One Scout attended a Jamboree in Japan and one a Jamboree in America in 1978. Scouts from the Group together with boys from the 19th Bromley Group formed the Plaistow Venture Unit, based in Bromley.

In 1980 the Group celebrated its Golden Jubilee and contact was made with various ex-members. The gathering was well attended and the ages of those present ranged from 16 to 83 years. An outstanding event during the year was a special service arranged by the vicar Rev. C K Channer. At about that time the Group won the Commissioner's Standard, the Cub Football Trophy, the Clay Aggregate Cup and the Scout Five-a-Side Trophy.

The strength of the Group in 1982 was 30 scouts and 42 cub scouts with a waiting list for boys wanting to become cub scouts. The leaders then were Ron Ridgway (Group Scout Leader); Ian Randall (Scout Leader); Mrs C Randall (Cub Scout Leader); Ian Harrington (Assistant Cub Scout Leader); and Instructors Mrs M Penney, Mr H Ludlam, Mr G Fuller and Mr A Elwood assisted by Ian Randall and Gary Fuller. Chris Jones became the Venture Scout leader assisted by Paul Bellinger and Denis Belcher.

A couple of years later David Justice, Chris Day and Martin Bellinger joined the troop as assistant leaders. Gloria Boon was Beaver leader from 1987/8 assisted by Barbara Belcher and Ros Denton. Sue Rushworth took over the reins in 1988, then in 1992 she became Akela assisted by Chris and Pauline Jones and Jane Hitchin. In 1988 Chris Jones took over as Group Scout Leader. Paul Bellinger and Paul Jones then ran the Venture Scout unit. Throughout this era the Penney family and the Justice family were active within the Group.

David Justice (Asst Scout Leader) and Jane Hitchin (Asst Cub Leader) married, as did Tony Elwood (Scout Leader) and Sue Rushworth (Cub Leader) in 2002.

In the early 1990s the 25th started a Beaver colony run, in the early years variously by Brenda Sharman, Sue Elwood (née Rushworth) assisted by Kate Allen and Steve White, and by Steve and Diane White and Heidi Malham.

Bruce Manning took over as Group Scout Leader around 2000 and is still serving in that role in 2012. At about the same time John Povey took over as Cub Scout Leader assisted by Emma Povey and Kevin Malham.

The scouts underwent an age range change which aligned scouting ages more towards school years. Scouts became 10-14 and Ventures then were renamed Explorers and the age range became 14-18 years. At the same time the 25th had its first female members joining all sections. In 2005 Paul Jones became the first Explorer Scout Leader of the 25th supported by Gary Fuller, Adam Panizzi and Adam Beacroft (one of the first 25th Beavers). Kate Allen then became an Explorer Leader in 2006 when Paul moved on. In 2012 Adam Panizzi is the leader supported by Gary Fuller, Kate Allen and Ben Callow (another boy to come up all the way through beavers). Kate was a Venture Scout and in 1993 became one of the first at the 25th to become Queen Scout Award holders, along with Edward Fevyer and Martin

Jones. Since then the ranks of Queen Scout Award holders include Adam Beacroft, Alex Bees, Cara Norman and Jenny Hodges.

John Povey took over as Scout Leader assisted by Tony Elwood, Ian Randall and Martin Bellinger and Dan Stimson joined in 2009. Emma Povey became Cub Scout Leader, assisted by Gary Hurle, Heidi Folley and Sam Povey.

With the Explorer Scouts, members of the group have cycled round the area of the Normandy landings, been skiing to France, chartered 3 yachts and sailed round the islands of Croatia as well as regular traditional camps to France, Jersey and Luxembourg.

The group, which is quite a family affair judging by the number of times the same surnames crop up, continues to be a hive of activity in the community.

15th and 7th Bromley Girl Guides

The 15th Bromley Company can trace its history back to the date of formation of the company in November 1926 at which time Miss M E Morris was the Captain and Miss M Sharpe Lieutenant.

The first mention of the Group in the annals of the church appeared in the Minutes for the St Andrew's Guild of Fellowship early in 1927 when the council voted an amount of £2 towards expenses and at the same meeting Mr Major agreed to present the company with their colours. For a short period in 1928 Miss O R Grey became Lieutenant and she was followed by Miss K M Bonny as Captain. According to the PCC Minutes of February 1929 the Captain was incapacitated as the result of a motor accident and had to hand over the running of the Group. The Group was served by a number of Captains and Lieutenants throughout the thirties and on through the war years. In the late forties and early fifties the Lieutenants appointed included Miss R Butler, Miss B M Ball, Mrs Geer and Mrs G Hunt. Mrs Hunt became Captain in 1952 and served for four years when Miss Doris Green took over responsibility for the Company serving, supported by Miss Alison Green, from 1959 until 1965, until 1967. Her place as Captain was taken by Miss Carol Bolton who remained as Captain for five years. In 1976 Mrs Nora MacMurray became Guide Captain.

The 7th Bromley Girl Guide Company was formed in 1958 under the captaincy of Mrs Olive Anderson.

During the '60s Miss Beryl Cooper and Miss Rosalind Clinch served as Lieutenants. Miss Annete Asher was appointed AGG in 1969 and Mrs Jean Griffiths served from

1970 until 1977. In 1978 Miss Jane Winteringham (later Mrs Cooper) became Captain and was joined in 1980 by Mrs Sheila Cox as AGG. From 1966 to 1982 the two companies affiliated to St Andrew's accumulate no less than eight Queen's Guide awards. The recipients were Debbie Cox and Caroline Davies (7th), and Linda Chinnery, Helen MacMillan, Jane Winteringham, Karen Forster, Hazel Ford and Clare Eldridge (15th).

Eventually the 7th Bromley moved to Brook Lane and the 15th company closed around 1992.

15th Bromley Brownies

The 15th Bromley Brownies were first registered in January 1933. Miss Maud Smith was the first Brown Owl and was followed by D Croft, Miss M E Arnaud, Mrs Margaret Kent, Miss Joyce E Ball, Mrs Blanche Sanderson, Miss Lucy I Largen, Mrs Sheila Pullen, Mrs Martin and Mrs Carol Luffman. The 15th Bromley has always been a very active pack. Miss Largen always took them on a pack holiday each year and Mrs Sheila Pullen involved them with community work such as keeping the church garden tidy, dusting the church, and working to keep the parade of shops in Burnt Ash Lane litter-free.

In the latter connection a march was organised through Bromley High Street with banners appealing to people to keep Britain tidy. Each Christmas the Brownies would sing carols to old folk in the Churchill Homes and at Bromley Hospital for the children. They took flowers to the occupants of St Andrew's House who were also invited to the Brownies' concert. The pack support the 'Blue Peter' appeals and joined other packs in the district for Brownie revels and swimming galas. They had a full programme including a Sports Day and visits to London, the coast and to France and Belgium. Each Brownie also gave 5p from her pocket money to go towards the education of a little girl overseas.

St Andrew's Cricket Club

St Andrew's Cricket Club existed, indeed flourished, within the first decade of the church's life. During the war years the blue caps could be admired on the Downham and Bellingham ground, and among the better known and most proficient wearers were Peter Garrett and the Rev. Michael Dittmer. The club most frequently recalled arose after the demise of the first and had a life of only six seasons (1947-1952) after which it was transformed into Ravensbourne Cricket Club.

Fig. 77 St Andrew's CC 1947.
Back row (L-R): 1 Bessie Bartholomew, 2 John Malcom Smith, 3 Brian (?), 4 David Harrison, 5 Ron Cason, 6 Bill Burford, 7 Roy Hadlow, 8 (?)
Front Row: 1 Derek Dickins, 2 Michael Bard, 3 Ron Gilbert

Initially the new SACC was no more than a group of friends who attended St Andrew's and shared a passion for cricket and, at its formation, none had reached the age of 20.

The greatest motivator was Bessie Bartholomew, Warden of the Guild of Service, who acted as secretary and umpire. The first captain was Ron Cason who, like a number of others, managed to combine National Service with regular club appearances.

One very successful season was 1948, with 12 out of 17 matches won - there might have been more but fixtures were often scratched at short notice. The team played at Queen's Mead when 'at home' and Roy Hadlow apart, was not over-strong in batting - a general weakness being an overweening ambition to clear the boundary. Bob Kemp and Ron Gilbert formed a useful and good looking opening pair but Roy was outstanding - a quick accumulator and in

Fig. 78 St Andrew's CC Approx 1951/2
Back Row (L-R):
1 (?), 2 John Cave, 3 John Malcolm Smith, 4 David Manning, 5 Gerald Freek .
Front Row: Douglas (?), 2 Bill Burford, 3 Bob Kemp, 4 David Harrison, 5 Anthony Harding

the mood a destroyer of most types of bowling. The St Andrew's attack was based largely on Cason and Hadlow, both unusually accurate and the former commanding pace rare in junior club cricket.

He could still collect most wickets at least cost when appearing in only a handful of August matches. Hadlow was a fine bowler, fast medium, but occasionally subject to spells of lassitude and self-doubt. Ron Gilbert had at least one season of delightful success with high-tossed alleged leg-breaks, and Bill Burford and David Harrison were more than useful in their respective styles.

The fielding, apart from Kemp's undemonstrative wicket-keeping, was enthusiastic but erratic. By 1950 six players were in the Forces, and Ron Cason at Kelham. New players tended to be recruited from the ranks of broken-voiced choristers and, over the years St Andrew's choir provided the likes of Bill Burford, Derek Dickins, Brian Wallace and David Jones.

Brian appeared but briefly and looked a complete cricketer. David was a real find, a bowler of pace and with suitable aggression,

Fig. 79 St Andrew's CC prior to 1953
Back row (L-R):
4 David Harrison, 5 Ron Gilbert, 6 Brian (?)
Front Row: 1 Derek Dickins, 2 Michael Bard, 3 Rev. W.T. Rees
4 Bryan Turner, 5 Geoff Payne (?)

but his triumphs were to be largely with Ravensbourne and Downham and Bellingham. In changeable circumstances the captains, Kemp, Gilbert and Michael Bard, had to be resourceful. The teams always played with an eye to victory but in attack, records show that they were heavily dependent on the availability of the original pace bowlers and Hadlow's batting could double an innings' total. Through all vicissitudes the team was invariably a happy one and, allowing for post-war austerities, well turned out.

The church connection had become less marked by 1952 but even the early Ravensbourne teams contained a number of regular St Andrew's communicants, and choir and servers provided a fair proportion of younger recruits. Joyful memories flood back for the middle-aged: Bob Kemp scoring a brisk fifty after an unaccustomed pint of draught cider; Ron Cason dismissing St James's, Elmers End twice in one afternoon aided only by the retreating movements of callow batsmen; Rev. S H Cooke on his one appearance at Queen's Mead producing a rasping square cut; Frank Jarvis driving once over an astonished wicketkeeper's head; Wickham Court requiring 7 runs with 7 wickets left and losing by 2 runs - the last three wickets being a unique hat-trick 'st Kemp b Gilbert'. Small wonder Michael Bard could write affectionate reminiscences to the 'Burning Bush' thirty years after the events and with all too few of the participants active in the game. Many of the players went on to play for years and with success in higher grade cricket, but that their devotion to the game lasted so long is in no small measure due to the happiness engendered in youthful days, and for which all of them would remember St Andrew's with lasting warmth.

Burnt Ash Drama Association

Burnt Ash Drama Association in 2011 celebrated its 50th birthday, but the history of the group goes back way beyond that, to the building of the church in 1930. At that time Mrs Lamb, later to become the first hall caretaker, was a leading light of the church's dramatic society, as was Daisy Syrett, who remained so, together with stalwarts such as Albert Anderson and Phyllis and Alan Barnett, until the early 1950s, when lack of members forced the group to close down.

For ten years St Andrew's had no drama group, but shortly after the arrival of choirmaster Malcolm Warwick, the group was reborn in 1961, with Pamela Warwick as the inspirational force.

The new St Andrew's Dramatic Society was just beginning to make an impact in local drama circles when the inadequacies of St Andrew's Hall forced the group's removal to St Augustine's Hall Grove Park. This was in 1967, and the next nine years were spent 'in exile'. St Andrew's standard continued to improve, however, helped immeasurably by Colin Oxenforth, St Andrew's curate from 1969-72, whose enthusiasm and talent communicated itself to existing members and the many new members he was able to introduce to the group. As a result of this improvement St Andrew's won the Bromley Festival in 1975 with its production of 'A Streetcar Named Desire', which also took third place in the Kent Festival.

It was in 1975 also that it was decided to change the name of the group to Burnt Ash Drama Association. There had been confusion between 'St Andrew's' and 'St Augustine's', where the group was then performing, and it was felt that the new name reflected more accurately its locality and membership. A year later the group returned to its old stamping ground of St Andrew's Hall, which was subsequently refurbished.

1978 was a notable year also, as it provided BADA with its first opportunity to perform at the Minack Theatre, Porthcurno, Cornwall. 'She Stoops to Conquer' was back to the theatre two years later, when the group's production of 'A Midsummer

Night's Dream' set up a Minack attendance record for the first week of the season.

Between these two productions, in 1979, BADA had scored another 'first', with 'Macbeth', its first Shakespeare presentation, and the first ever to be staged in the church hall. The group had by this time established itself as one of the leading groups in Bromley, and in 1980 and 1981 won the Bromley Festival with 'Ghosts' by Ibsen and 'The Long and the Short and the Tall' by Willis Hall.

Continuing its policy of presenting more and more challenging plays BADA staged 'Hedda Gabler' by Ibsen and 'A View from the Bridge' by Arthur Miller. While neither production won any major honours in the two festivals in which they were entered, they demonstrated the strength and dedication of a group which has come a long way from the genial amateurishness of its early days.

Burnt Ash Drama Association (BADA for short) has been established in its present form for 50 years. However the current highly-regarded, prolific award-winning group evolved from the no less talented St Andrew's (Bromley) Dramatic Society, which had been in limbo since 1951 until being re-formed 10 years later with the arrival of a new choirmaster at St Andrew's. His wife (Pamela Warwick), Bill Burford (multi-faceted actor, producer, director, stage manager and one-time BADA chairman over the years until bowing out in the mid-90s), Arthur Short (design brains behind many of the company's productions, as well as a more than capable stage manager) and actor/producer Cyril Wallace, a research chemist at Woolwich Arsenal, were the inspiration behind the revived group, which was to continue under its previous name for several more years.

The society's nine-strong first production, on which one local newspaper commented that "the company showed from the first that they were no novice hands" and "the teamwork was excellent" was *Quiet Weekend*, a comedy by Esther McCracken. All four of the above-mentioned founder members took main roles, along with another young founding member, Andrew Martin.

Arthur, Bill and Cyril went on to become regular features of the group, which even made headlines in London in 1966 when the members put on David Turner's *Semi-Detached*, in its day considered a daring satire on modern morals. Father Peter Cole at St Andrew's backed the production, leading to a story in the *Evening Standard* headed "Vicar defends sex-theme play"! (As an aside, an annual subscription that year would have set you back 10 shillings – or five shillings for members still at school ....)

From 1967 until 1975, the society, whilst still rehearsing at St Andrew's Hall in Burnt Ash Lane, had to find a new home because the hall had no performing licence. So, in order to put on such diverse productions as *The Happiest Days of Your Life*, *On Monday Next* (where one critic said: "Despite being 'homeless', the society goes from strength to strength") and *The Crucible*, Bill and Cyril and rising stars such as Mair Lloyd-Roberts kept the flag flying at St Augustine's Hall in Grove Park.

In 1969, St Andrews took the plunge, entering the first of what were to be innumerable numbers of drama festivals over the ensuing years, bringing in their wake a sackful of well-merited awards. Their initial entry was Ian Stuart Black's *We Must Kill Toni*, a three-act murder play entered in the Kent & Bromley Drama Festival. On this occasion, the company didn't win any awards, although Bill (whose wife, Jill, incidentally, played the eponymous Toni) was given an honourable mention by the adjudicator.

Bill had a little more success two years later, when *The Winslow Boy*, produced by the Rev. Colin Oxenforth, earned him a Runner-Up Best Actor award in the Bromley Theatre Guild Drama Festival, alongside Arthur Short and Richard Matthews for Best Set. This production also had some significance as it was Mair Lloyd-Roberts' debut with the company. She herself went on to win shelves-ful of acting, directing and best production awards and indeed is still doing so, and is the only actress in the area to have received 6 Best Actress Awards. Bill's considerable thespian talents were recognised the following year when he and Cyril (later to become BADA president) received joint Best Actor awards in the festival for their roles in *The Crucible*, which another of the organisation's talented thespians, Anne-Marie Martin, produced. The play won Runner-Up Best Production, with Dick Jefferis gaining Best Small-Part Actor award.

The year 1975 proved a significant turning point for the St Andrew's members. Having harvested a whole host of awards in the Bromley Guild Festival for its production of *A Streetcar Named Desire* (gaining a place in the finals of the Kent Drama Festival, where Bill was Runner-Up Best Actor), the company changed its name to its present title and, licence granted, returned to its home in St Andrew's Hall. The first production under its new mantle was Neil Simon's *Plaza Suite*, with each of the three playlets having a separate producer. Then in 1977 BADA made local drama history by putting on the plague-based *The Roses of Eyam* in St Andrew's Church. This was a huge undertaking requiring a cast of 50+ and BADA was supplemented by church members for the occasion.   BADA has never shirked at taking on such challenges, and the following year saw the members involved in another: the first of several visits over the years to the striking open-air Minack Theatre, hewn out of the rocks on the Cornish coast, beginning with *She Stoops To Conquer*. Subsequent productions have included *A Midsummer Night's Dream*, *London Assurance* and Tom Stoppard's *On The Razzle*.

As former BADA actor/producer Andrea Gambell told the press: "The atmosphere of the place is magical. As a performer you feel as if you have the audience in the palm of your hand – as if you were somehow able to manipulate them. It's a very special feeling."

Meanwhile, the company was still picking up major awards, which indeed it continues to do in its fiftieth year. *Ghosts* won the 1980 Bromley Guild festival, as did *The Long and The Short and The Tall* the following year. In 1984, *The Dresser,* with current chairman David Evans (who joined BADA in 1982 for *Hedda Gabler* and is no stranger to acting and directing, not to mention countless awards, himself, being the only actor in the area to have achieved 7 Best Actor Awards) in the title role, reached the finals of the Kent Drama Festival.

In 1988, BADA entered new territory. Not content with enthralling the denizens of Penzance, they made the first of several subsequent forays to Spain. At the cosy Salon de Varietes theatre in Fuengirola, they treated the expats to the delights of cricketing comedy *Outside Edge*, which was well received. Eight more productions, amongst them, *Murder on The Nile*, *Dancing At Lughnasa*, *The Country Wife* and an ambitious *Nicholas Nickleby* followed by demand.

In St Andrew's Hall, meanwhile, a succession of acclaimed dramas, farces, comedies – and even the odd musical – have continued to bring in the audiences whatever the weather. In 2008 the society won the first of a hat-trick of victories in the Bromley Full Length Play Festival with *David Copperfield*, followed in 2009 by *The Government Inspector* and again in 2010 the stunning production of *The Grapes Of Wrath*, which swept the board with its awards – all directed by the current Chairman David Evans. Long-standing BADA president Joan Harris must be a happy lady. As Andrea Gambell said in the interview, which still holds today: "It would be easy to fall back on potboilers, but we've always tried to put on plays that are above par and hopefully will continue to do so".

The Adventurers

The Adventurers, formerly known as the King's Messengers, is an organisation for children, which exists to support the United Society for the Propagation of the Gospel in their work for the church overseas.

The Annual Report of the church for the year 1932 records that a branch of the King's Messengers had been started and 1982 marked the Golden Jubilee for the group at St Andrew's. In their early days the King's Messengers met under the leadership of Miss Jenkin-Jones. Meetings are believed to have ceased during the war as the minutes of the church annual meeting of 1948 mention that, the King's Messengers branch had been revived after a lapse of some years and that groups of boys and girls were now working for the church overseas'. The sale for that year raised £2/3s for SPG funds. At that time the leadership was in the hands of Miss Phyllis Barnet and Mr E Saville. Mr and Mrs Saville left the parish in 1955 but the group carried on and has continued to flourish under the dedicated leadership of several St Andrew's people including Florence and Arthur Short, Frank Jarvis and Elsie Burford. The Group was run from 1973 by Mrs Doreen Viner and under her leadership and over a ten-year period the children of the Adventurers raised over £1300 most of which went to missions overseas with the hall fund benefiting from the balance.

The Friends of St Andrew's

'The Friends' was formed in 1991 on an initiative of Fr Anthony Atherton as a focus for fund-raising in aid of the upkeep, maintenance and improvement of the church and hall buildings and grounds. It was set up as a charity (Reg. No.1004168) and since that time it has been run by a small committee partly appointed by the PCC and partly elected at the annual meeting of the charity. Up until 2011 it had raised over £65,000, spent £20,000 on various projects and allocated a substantial sum towards the building of the much needed new St Andrew's community hall.

Brook Lane Chapel

The Downham Estate was named after Lord Downham, the then Chairman of the London County Council, and was not complete at the time Brook Lane Hall was opened in 1928. Previously it had been possible to walk over seven fields past Shroffold Farm to Southend Pond and footwear became covered with white dust or mud whilst traversing Whitefoot Lane. Before the Hall was opened a missionary at home on furlough from Argentina visited houses in the Rangefield Road area and invited women to a Women's Fellowship held in a house in Park Avenue. The convenor of these meetings was a member of a Christian Brethren Church in Bromley.

The friends from this Church and a similar group in Catford bought a plot of land in Brook Lane and erected a building in which the Gospel could be proclaimed. The Women's Fellowship was transferred to the newly built hall and a Sunday School was opened. About 500 children gathered, teachers taking a session for boys, followed by one for girls; a Primary Class was also held, in a room at the back of the

Hall. Many people attended Gospel Services and special evangelistic campaigns resulted in a number of conversions to the Christian faith. Thus a local Church was established in Brook Lane Hall.

The Christian witness developed and it became necessary to erect an additional Hall on the same plot. Subsequently two groups 'hived off' to establish local Christian Brethren Churches, first on the Mottingham Estate and then on the Whitefoot Estate. Further expansion occurred as missionary interest sent dedicated young people to central and North Africa to make Christ known. Concern for the Gospel outreach worldwide continues to this day.

The story of "Brook Lane" would be incomplete without grateful reference to the Brook Lane and Bermondsey Medical Mission which also uses the premises. Dr B G Morton, OBE and the late Sister Swain who were working in the Bermondsey area felt the need to commence medical work amongst the Bermondsey families who had moved to Downham, and in 1937 a Medical Mission was started in Brook Lane Hall, now known as Brook Lane Chapel. Since that time the doctors and staff have ministered to the physical and spiritual needs of many in Downham, Mottingham and other parts of Bromley, as well as in Bermondsey. Brook Lane Hall was emblazoned with inviting words "Hall of the warm welcome" and today Brook Lane Chapel members seek under God's hand to maintain this high standard'.

Rangefield Mission

Rangefield Mission opened its doors to the populace of the Downham Estate on 10th October 1933. A commemorative plaque in the Hall announced that it was erected for the Glory of God, and that the building was opened by the Earl of Shaftesbury as Patron of the Shaftesbury Society.

As far back as 1927 a group of young committed Christians had seen the need for a Mission on the Estate. They went to various Churches in Bromley, and Mr Cyril Sherriff had the vision or foresight to gather together those who were ready and able and they started open-air meetings on the Greens on the Downham Estate; this led to Sunday Schools and meetings in houses, and finally, when the project got too large, they rented accommodation in Burnt Ash School. By this time it was obvious that a permanent home was needed and The Shaftesbury Society agreed to meet part of the cost of the building if Mr Sherriff and his friends could raise the rest of the money. They succeeded, and Rangefield Mission came into being.

During the years before the War in 1939 the numbers in the congregation grew - to the extent that if you did not get there early you might not get a seat! There were Girls and Boys Brigades, mid-week Bible classes, and nearly 200 children in the Sunday School. During the War the Mission remained open. They held their services in the afternoons and if necessary used the air-raid shelters at the school opposite. In those early days there were many "underprivileged', children on the Estate. Cars were almost unheard of, and those who did own cars were looked on with awe. Radios were a luxury and TV had not been invented. There was nowhere else for people to go. The Annual outing to the seaside - nearly always Margate - was very often the only opportunity the children had of going to the sea. With a brief experimental interval in the 1950s when there was a paid pastor (Mr J Mackenzie-Forbes) Mr Sherriff remained as voluntary superintendent until his death in 1972 at the age of 92. Since then several pastors were provided by the Shaftesbury Society.

The Shaftesbury Society was founded 170 years ago by the Earl of Shaftesbury to provide education and better conditions for the poor children of London and ran Urban Missions (Free Churches) and homes for disadvantaged children, especially for children with Spinabifida, Muscular Dystrophy and Multiple Sclerosis.

In 2007 two charities John Grooms and the Shaftesbury Society merged to form Livability founded on a Christian ethos to provide services to disabled people at home and abroad.

The mission finally closed and became the site of four new houses but one small but important item from the mission survived. A memorial plaque commemorating four servicemen connected with the mission who fell in the Second Work War was recovered from the site and given to St Andrew's for safe keeping. This has now taken its rightful place alongside the Wayside Shrine and Remembrance Book in St Andrew's church in perpetuity (see Ch 8).

Bromley and Downham Youth Club

Just within the western boundary of St Andrew's parish is that hive of Activity, the Bromley and Downham Youth Club. The club was first set up of the Canterbury, Oxford & Bermondsey Mission as the Bromley and Downham Boys' Club. Its theme was to provide recreational facilities, cultural and spiritual aid to the boys on the estate.

In 1934 the premises in Valeswood Road were opened and consisted of a games room, a Chapel, a very small kitchen, a small billiard room, a small gymnasium, boiler room with a shower, a lavatory, and a very small office. In 1949 the club was handed over to the then Mayor of Bromley Alderman B J Finnie MC. Mr Lew Ashman was appointed club leader. Activities included sports, handicrafts, camping, and many indoor activities. Throughout the years the club developed into an integral centre of the community as well as gaining honours in sport and the arts. Time brought its ups and downs with many changes in leadership and personnel and, in the early sixties went through a testing period with the leadership eventually becoming part-time. In 1965, the Chairman of the club, Mr Frank Warwick, appointed a new full-time leader, Mr Pat Matthews, who served until 1978. In 1982 the chairman was Roy Higgs and the club leader Mike Raybold.

In 1969, with government and local authority aid, the first major development took place. The old communal air raid shelter was demolished, a floodlit play area was opened, lavatories, changing rooms and showers were installed, the old coke boiler removed and gas heating laid on. The club had to raise a sum in excess of £3,000 as its contribution to the venture. In the same year, girl members were admitted to the club for the first time on two evenings a week. The club continued to develop its wide range of activities and interests. Membership continued to rise and more emphasis was placed on serving the community. Unattached youngsters was being catered for, with the club house becoming a centre where help and advice with problems could be dealt with. Parents as well as the youngsters used these facilities. The old and infirm were not forgotten with members carrying out many tasks to help them and the annual Party and Pantomime became an established date in the calendar.

In 1971 there was a major development when, with the help of the London Federation of Boys Clubs and the generosity of the Joseph Levy Charitable Foundation, the new sports hall was built and structural alterations made which provided a coffee bar, workshop, table tennis room and additional storage space. The new facilities were opened by Prince Philip in July of that year. The club is now open 4 evenings a week (Monday to Thursday) offering young people between the ages of 8 – 18 (older for boxers and SEN (Special Educational Needs)) a variety of activities including sports, IT, art and song and dance.

The boxing section runs 3 nights a week on Monday, Tuesday and Thursday. There is now also a Special Educational Needs (SEN) Group who meet on a Wednesday. The staff are part-time, trained as youth workers (including an ABA boxing coach) and supported by a team of volunteers on Management Committee and Trustees. The young people can try out new activities and achieve accreditation for what they do. Off-site activities are also run selectively, taking member groups to country wide venues to experience outdoor activities.

Being situated on the borders of both Bromley and Lewisham, the club is involved with both Boroughs and are members of both Voluntary Action Lewisham and Bromley Council of Voluntary Youth Services .

The club receives some funding from the London Boroughs of Bromley and Lewisham but insufficient to meet all outgoings. It is affiliated to London Youth who also support some of the staff training.

The building is on two levels; downstairs there is a purpose built Sports Hall and another smaller hall, upstairs there is office space, kitchen, workshop, art room and IT suite. With need to expand our boxing section space we now have a new purpose built sports hall, which will also allow the club to offer fitness training. The new development also included fully accessible toilets and showers and new chairlift and was opened by HRH the Duke of Edinburgh on 22nd May 2012 this being his second visit to the club.

Fig. 80 HRH The Duke of Edinburgh at the opening of the newly developed club facility.

(L-R) Leah Crawley, Head Teacher, Burnt Ash Primary School, Sharon Grange, Head Teacher, St Josephs RC Primary School, George Taylor (Front), Hilary Cheverton, Trustee, Bromley and Downham Youth Club (Behind the Duke's right shoulder), Amanda Dixson, Leader in Charge, Bromley and Downham Youth Club (R)

Photo: Tony Isbitt Photography

Moving the boxing section into the new facility has enabled the club to release the small downstairs hall which is now used exclusively by Blossom Years Pre-School.

Plans are in hand to extend opening times to include day time opening for the local community such as Mother and Toddler Coffee Bar Pop-in, Youth Persons HUB and Zumba and Slimming World and to extend the existing Short Mat Bowling.

More recent developments have included the affiliation of the Boxing Section to the London Amateur Boxing Association, the opening of a Karate Section and a junior section for boys and girls aged from six to ten. Other sections continuing to flourish are hobbies, football, trampolining, weight training and girls' netball and badminton.

The undeniable success of the club owes much to the dedication of countless members of the management team, who over many years have steered the club through thick and thin. It has become an institution without which the community of Downham would be much the poorer .

Fig. 81 HRH The Duke of Edinburgh talking to Rev. Angela King and Rev. Elizabeth Davis

Photo: Tony Isbitt Photography

Appendix II
St Andrew's Church, Bromley

List of Incumbents

1927-1940	Rev. J MT Griffiths MA
1940-1950	Rev. S H Cooke, BA
1950-1964	Rev. W T Rees Lic.Div.
1965-1972	Rev. P G L Cole, MA
1972-1974	Rev. P Hinchey LTCL
1975-1981	Rev. C K Channer BD, AKC
1982-1987	Rev. Cannon Gordon O'Loughlin MA
1987-2011	Rev. H A Atherton MA, BSc, FGS

List of Priests in Charge

1942-1945	Rev. R W Walls AKC
1945-1946	Rev. K T Makin
2011 -	Rev. A King BA (Hons), Dip.Ed.,Dip. Theol.

List of Curates

1939-1941	Rev. N D Walker
1941-1943	Rev. M W Dittmer BA (Oxon)
1966-1969	Rev. Adrian Vivian BD, AKC
1969-1972	Rev. Colin Oxenforth BA, Dip. Th.

List of Assistant and Hon. Assistant Priests

1938-1940	Rev. R J W Grindle AKC
1943-1945	Rev. R H Rice BA, L Th.
1964	Rev. P Duffett MA Dip. Th.
1964-1965	Rev. D N Griffiths MA (Hon. Asst Curate)
1969-1973	Rev. I A L Little ARICS
1973-?	Rev. B Kaenel
1979-1994	Rev. F Heydon AKC
1983-1986	Rev. N Bunker BD, AKC
1998-	Rev. E. Davis

List of Churchwardens

Year	Vicar's Warden	People's Warden	Year	Vicar's Warden	People's Warden	Year	Vicar's Warden	People's Warden
1927	Mr F H Sheriff	Mr C Sheldon	1949	Mr C E Clarke	Mr H Syrett	1971	Mr K C W Evans	Mr P A I Dulley
1928	"	"	1950	"	"	1972	"	Mr C E Clarke
1929	"	"	1951	Mr C E Turner	"	1973	Mr N Warner	"
1930	"	"	1952	"	"	1974	"	Mr F Ollive
1931	"	"	1953	"	"	1975	Mr M W Hall	"
1932	"	"	1954	"	"	1976	"	Mr C G Wallace
1933	Mr T H Kenyon	Mr F H Sheriff	1955	"	"	1977	"	"
1934	"	"	1956	"	"	1978	Mr L A Rackham	"
1935	"	Mr O J Sprinks	1957	"	"	1979	Miss E Clarke	"
1936	"	"	1958	"	"	1980	"	"
1937	"	"	1959	"	"	1981	"	Mr C G Wallace
1938	"	"	1960	"	"	1982	"	"
1939	"	"	1961	"	"	1983	"	"
1940	"	Mr H Syrett	1962	"	"	1984	"	"
1941	Mr F Wise	"	1963	"	Mr F Chappell	1985	"	"
1942	"	"	1964	"	Mr F J Stanger	1986	Mr M W Hall	Mrs M Gelhespy
1943	Mr C E Clarke	"	1965	"	"	1987	"	"
1944	"	"	1966	Mr C E Clarke	"	1988	"	"
1945	"	"	1967	"	"	1989	Mrs M Gelhespy	Mrs J Barnes
1946	"	"	1968	"	Mr A H Dalton	1990	"	"
1947	"	"	1969 *	"	"	1991	Mr A J Martin	Mr P A I Dulley
1948	"	"	1970	Mr K C W Evans	Mr A H Dalton	1992	"	"

* After 1969 it ceased to be the custom for the incumbent to nominate a 'vicar's warden'. Thereafter, both wardens were elected at the Annual Vestry Meeting.

List of Churchwardens

Year	Vicar's Warden	People's Warden	Year	Vicar's Warden	People's Warden	Year	Vicar's Warden	People's Warden
1993	Mr A J Martin	Mr P A I Dulley	2000	Mr D justice	Mrs A King	2007	Mr D justice	Mrs D Williams
1994	"	"	2001	"	Mr J Hassall	2008	"	"
1995	"	"	2002	"	"	2009	"	"
1996	"	Mr D Barton-Marshall	2003	"	"	2010	"	Mr M Turner
1997	Miss T Dulley		2004	"	"	2011	"	"
1998	"	Mrs A King	2005	"	Mrs D Williams	2012	"	"
1999	"	"	2006	"	"			

List of List of Organists and Choirmasters

1925-1953	Mr H G Woodhams LLCM (TD), LTSC	1968-1972	Mr N Osborne FRCO, GRSM, LRAM, ARCM
1953-1955	Mr R J Keefe*	1973-1975	Mr A Taylor GRSM, ARCO (CHM), LTCL, ARCM
1955-1958	Mr R Cooper*	1975-1983	Mr A H J Knight (Choirmaster) Mrs S A Knight (Organist)
1958-1959	Mr E A Bloomfield LTCL, L Mus.TCL, LRAM, ARCO	1985-1986	Mr G Frost*
1959-1964	Mr M F Warwick*	1994-1997	Mr D Barton-Marshall*
1965-1966	Mr G E Henley*	1998-2007	Mr P Moore*
1966-1968	Mr D F Hammond FTCL, LRAM, ARCM, FRCA	2011-	Mrs Gloria Toplis BMus, MMus, GRSM, LRAM, ARAM

*At the time of going to press, diplomas have not been traced

List of List of Lay Readers

1925-1948	Mr B G Parkerson	1966-1969	Mr A S Anderson

Appendix III
St Mary's Church, Bromley

List of Incumbents

1863-1867	Rev. Reuben Graham BA
1867-1871	Rev. Sir Louis Hesketh Fleetwood Bart, BA
1871-1873	Rev. Alfred J. Myers BA
1873-1898	Rev. William Hodgson MA
1898-1904	Rev. John Bond MA
1904-1908	Rev. Edward Lotherington Colebrooke MA
1908-1937	Rev. William Gowans MA
1937-1942	Rev. Walter Richard Crichton MA
1942-1948	Rev. Patrick Powell Kirwin BA
1948-1959	Rev. John Hermann Rahe-Hughes BA
1959-1971	Rev. William Angus MacFarlane MA
1971-1997	Rev. Peter Henwood MA
1998-2005	Rev Simon Burton-Jones MA, BTh
2006-	Rev Alan Keeler BSc, DPS, MA

List of Curates

1883-1884	Rev. H A Thorne
1884-1889	Rev. E C Baldwin
1889-1898	Rev. H.F. Maltby
1898-1903	Rev. M C Wells
1898-1900	Rev. W S Flynn
1901-1905	Rev. C A Curgenven
1903-1905	Rev. H Curgenven
1905-1909	Rev. C de R Wall
1905-1906	Rev. C H Muspratt
1906-1908	Rev. F H Thomas
1908-1911	Rev. E H Lord
1909-1911	Rev. C B Sellwood
1911-1913	Rev. H W L Snow
1911-1913	Rev. T Leigh Jones
1913-1914	Rev. G O Morgan Smith
1914	Rev. C E Payne
1914-1915	Rev. J R O'Rourke
1915-1918	Rev. F H Manser
1919-1920	Rev. M P Shipman
1920-1925	Rev. C C W Cooper
1926	Rev. F G Hall
1928-1930	Rev. J W St A Davies
1925-1926	Rev. G E Parsons
1932	
1956-1959	Rev. R Vick
1965-1969	Rev. D Chaning-Pearce
1970-1972	Rev. J W Tipping
1976-1979	Rev. R Wallace
1979-1982	Rev. A Gorham
1982-1985	Rev. R Cotton
1986-1990	Rev. L Kevis
1993-1994	Rev. G Colville
1994-1995	Rev. E Davis
1996-1999	Rev. G Lloyd
1999-2000	Rev. S Young
2011-	Rev. G Burnett-Chetwynd

Bibliography

Atkinson, Capt. C T	*The Queen's Own Royal West Kent Regiment 1914-1919*
Hart, F H	*History of Lee and its Neighbours (1882)*
Hasted, Edward	*The History and Topographical Survey of the County of Kent, Published 1797-1801*
Horsburgh E L S	*Bromley, Kent - From the Earliest Times to the Present Century*
Knowlden, Patricia	*The Long Alert 1937 -1945*
MacFarlane, Rev. Angus	*St Mary's First Hundred Years 1863-1963*
Molony, Major C V	*"Invicta" With the 1st Battalion The Queen's Own Royal West Kent Regiment in the Great War*
Wilson, Thos	*An accurate description of Bromley (1797)*

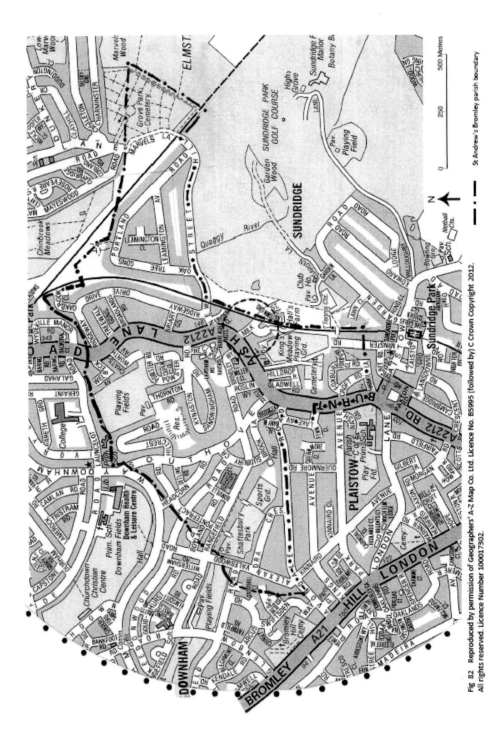

St Andrew's Bromley parish boundary

A Mile from Milk Street

Not a Mile from Milk Street Quiz.

Fig 83   Burnt Ash Primary School Class Photo 1957

In order to win the prize, you have to be the first to identify all the characters in the picture, including the teacher, and state which of them carved out an international career on the music scene.

Answers including name and address to:-

admin@burntash.bromley.sch.uk

I am indebted to Trish Rosel, Melbourne, Australia (formerly Pat Martin) for the photo in which she appears somewhere.

Index

To reference names only

147